T0106071

Snapshots

Snapshots

Sixty-Six Books of the Bible:

A Devotional

Earl Fashbaugh

Trafford Publishing

Trafford rev. 08/02/2011

 www.trafford.com

North America & international
toll-free: 1 888 232 4444 (USA & Canada)
phone: 250 383 6864 ♦ fax: 812 355 4082

To my family, now and to come

If anyone loves me, he will obey my teaching. My Father will love him, and we will come to him and make our home with him. He who does not love me will not obey my teaching. These words you hear are not my own; they belong to the Father who sent me.

Jesus Christ

John 14: 23, 24 (Life Application Study Bible, NIV)

Table of Contents

<u>Purpose</u>

Before the days of digital technology we carried around cheap cameras to various vacation spots, family gatherings, or special events like birthdays. Our closets would become congested, not only with our own pictures, but with those of family members who may have long since passed away. We stare at the pictures and memories are conjured up. Perhaps we can recall the entire day from a single picture; we feel the fall breeze and the promise of another season. Perhaps we recall how we dressed our children up for a picture and how they fussed about the entire ordeal. Maybe we can even smell the old jacket that our loved one wore as we stare at the faded colors on the small representation of the person who is captured by the snapshot. The ambitious few take time to put them in a photo album in some kind of chronology.

"Snapshots" is a kind of verbal photo album that uses the 66 books of the Bible as a catalyst to move our thoughts to each of these portions of scripture. Just as a photograph of days gone by does not capture the entire event, neither does this devotional expand the entire meaning or application for any single book in the Bible. Taking a picture, or snapshot, of a moment does not really do justice for a beautiful scene we witnessed during our vacation, but it puts a stake in our mind. The picture may even suggest that we have experienced something grand and we want to go back and visit the vacation spot again. We will always find something new when we re-visit scripture.

The Bible is relational in style in that it speaks to us in a personal way. So, when we start taking our own snapshots of the Bible, we charter the important scenes that relate to us at that particular time in life. Every day in this devotional is dedicated to a book in the Bible, 66 days in all. The devotional alternates old and New Testament books until the New Testament is "all used up" and then the Old Testament rounds out the later portion of the devotional. The book of Revelation is an exception and is last (Day 66). As the Bible is relational, the author provides his own verbal pictures of the first part of each book, illustrating the application according to his experience. The reader is then challenged to take the passage and pray about it and then find a meaning that is unique to them. If the Holy Spirit is in control, there will be no wrong answers to the questions in life that constantly provoke us to cry out for God to explain the snapshot of our lives.

I have tried to build into this devotional the subject matter of growth and maturity. The avenue to maturity is bumpy and we sometimes experience set-backs. It is hoped that those who read these words already recognize that sin causes set-backs. If per chance the reader does not believe in sin or most of the concepts presented in the Bible, they are challenged to put the Bible to the test.

The collection of books we call the Bible came into being in 383AD and has been scrutinized for authenticity since the first Latin version came into existence. But, regardless of this scrutiny we have based laws and morality on the words printed in the Bible. In addition, we are given messages that are of Devine nature if we truly seek to find the truth of the universe applied to our life and day-to-day problems.

When we take a photograph from a valley, we get a different perspective than if we take a picture from a mountain top. Note that the valley and the corresponding mountain may not be very far apart. But, if we stand in a valley our view may be obstructed, compared to an elevated point of observation. So it is with our perspective on life. Our distance to the highest hill of exuberance and total joy may not be very far from the low areas of depression and despair. Sometimes we can adjust where we stand to take the snapshot of our lives. In other cases, we cannot change our situation. How do we handle that? The hope is that each "snapshot" illustrates a hill or valley situation and provides a view from the mountain. However, it is up to the reader of the Bible to create their own "photo album." The questions and illustrations in this book are only from the perspective of an author who has lived in both the valley and the mountain.

Introduction

The Bible was written for us to read (or have someone read to us) and not for someone else to tell us what it says. Although it is true that every word in the Bible has a literal meaning, a deeper application is very personal. We can learn from Bible scholars and should be extremely grateful for those who carry academic credentials which earn them the right to serve as Pastors, Ministers, Priests, and Lay-pastors. But, we must take it on ourselves to sit quietly and read, pray, and contemplate the application of the Bible to our everyday lives.

Every book in the Bible is relevant and has a significant place holder in God's message to us. We could spend a lifetime studying individual books of the Bible but the fact is, most of us will not study the Bible in minute detail but we should hunger to touch every part of the Bible because it exists for our instruction, benefit, guidance, and encouragement.

One evening, I was studying an assignment for adult Sunday School. We were in the first chapter of Genesis. Suddenly, I discovered something really wonderful and I felt compelled to write it down – to take a snapshot of what the scripture meant to me. The next day, I felt equally compelled to read a New Testament Book, starting with Matthew. The same wonderful thing happened and I was compelled to write something down about the meaning of the scripture at that particular moment in life. The Holy Spirit seemed to keep prodding, "go ahead and write that down." I took a flying vacation through the Bible, quickly taking snapshots and recording a piece of myself along the way.

After embarking on this exercise, I realized that the scripture was written on a personal level. Please read this devotional with your Bible besides you. Realize that the "focus scripture" that I used was personal and that personal applications are waiting for you. What inspires you will probably be entirely different than what triggered the spiritual shutter for me. If my observations do not relate to you, that is probably because God has something else more important to say to you, personally.

God has left us a Love letter and instruction manual. See if you can hone in on those spiritual muscles that have been sedentary for a while. In essence, you will be writing your own journal and responding to God's personal inspiration if you write down a few notes at the end of each reading. What is important is not how I was moved by the scripture, but how the Spirit moves the reader into a place of peace and understanding. A devotional is only as good as the quality time put into it. For some, early morning is the best time to dedicate time to read the Bible. For others, early evening is ideal but rarely is bedtime a good time to feel the full energy and dynamic power of God's Word. Just put your fingers on the shutter and take 66 pictures of your own.

Day 1: The Us for us

Scripture–Genesis: Chapter 1

When we say, "Let's go" we anticipate a change as we decide that one task is done and another is on the horizon. When we plan our day, we tend to organize it in pieces like sections of a fence. One board at a time is nailed in place but what if the carpenter of the universe wanted us to see the work from outside the yard rather than inside the fence. That is the message waiting for us in Genesis where we realize that we are given a chance to be a part of His construction project.

Focus Scripture: Genesis 1:14, 15

And God said, "Let there be lights in the expanse of the sky to separate the day from the night, and let them serve as signs to mark seasons and days and years, and let them be lights in the expanse of the sky to give light on the earth." And it was so.

Focus Scripture: Genesis 1:26

"Let us make man in **Our** image, according to **Our** likeness; and let them rule …"

Focus Scripture: Genesis 11:7 (getting a little ahead of the story)

"Come let Us go down and there confuse their language, that they may not understand one another's speech."

The first focus scripture deals with the energy and detail of our physical universe. The total thermal and light energy of the universe is in equilibrium but is dissipating. The laws of thermodynamics are constant unless interrupted by God the Creator but most scientists attest to an ultimate beginning, regardless of how God initially designed everything.

The second focus scripture refers to God creating man and woman, a positive action that makes us feel secure. God was done with one part of creation and was on to another–creating us in His image. What a wonderful act of love! The second focus scripture does not leave us with such a secure feeling. Mankind was launching a "let go of God" campaign after God had invited us to participate in a "Let's go" plan. The boundaries were defined by God who provided a fenced pasture for us to enjoy. It follows that when we try to alter the course designed by the fence maker, we end up wandering around in utter confusion, not understanding God or ourselves.

Who is the "Us" in these scriptures? It is God, The Holy Spirit, and His Son, inseparable, all knowing, and all loving. This is the "Us for us" message to humankind, as if to say "We could just be Us but we want to share this with you." This is the grace of Genesis, that God and His Son, Jesus, were there, together, right from the beginning. There are other references to God as "Us" and "We" throughout scripture and the wonderful truth is that we are not alone when we go somewhere or do something. Sometimes I say to myself "let's pick up the kids" or "let's see if we can find my wife." What am I talking about? There is only me by myself, isn't there? Wrong. The Holy Spirit is right there with us, offering to be a part of the decision making process.

How do you see your own life plan organized right now? Is your perspective different than it was five years ago and how so?

Is there any other passage that strikes you in a personal manner (i.e. is there something written that you can especially relate to)?

2

Did you ever get the feeling that God surveyed the land before building the structure of your life?

Write down a short prayer of thanksgiving for His plan.

Day 2: Who's the Father?

Scripture–Matthew: Chapter 1

Quite frankly, family trees do not interest me very much. But that may be because I have so little information about my own ancestry. I read this portion of scripture to my family after supper and the kids wondered if it would ever end. But, clearly this ancestry was very important to Matthew. For some, the long list of descendants, starting with Abraham, then David, and finally Jesus, is a tedious and maybe trivial portion of scripture. Truth is, the family tree lives on and will continue into end times. As foretold by Isaiah, the prophesy was fulfilled by the birth, the nature of birth, and the life of Jesus. Just as David would emerge from his humble responsibility of following sheep and leading sheep, the great Shepard, Jesus would rise up from the work bench and lead the world to a place where we would be called heirs to God. But not only is it important for us to realize the fulfillment of prophesy–it is imperative that we realize the means of conception. The Daddy of Jesus is the Holy Spirit, and this miracle is a cornerstone of our beliefs.

But, imagine how we would react if we were confronted with the knowledge that our fiancé became pregnant by someone else. How would we respond?

Focus Scripture: Matthew 1:19

And Joseph her husband, being a righteous man, and not wanting to disgrace her, desired to put her away secretly.

5

Focus Scripture: Matthew 1:22, 23

All this took place to fulfill what the Lord had said through the prophet: "The virgin will be with child and will give birth to a son, and they will call him Immanuel" which means, "God with us."

Focus Scripture: Matthew 1:25

...and kept her a virgin until she gave birth to a son; and he called His name "Jesus."

Perhaps a modern dialogue between Joseph and a friend might follow this pattern:

Joseph: Bob, I haven't told anyone but Mary is pregnant.

Bob: Oh, hey, sorry to hear that. You guys were going to get married soon anyway.

Joseph: Yeah, but Bob, she isn't pregnant by me.

Bob: That's bad news. So, are you going to dump her?

Joseph: No, listen to me. She's a virgin; the Holy Spirit is the father. Really, Bob, you have to believe me.

Bob: I don't know what she told you but as far as I am concerned, she is trash.

At this point Bob reels backwards as Joseph connects with a sharp jab to the nose. Minutes later Joseph is still holding an ice pack over his friend's face.

Joseph: I'm sorry I lost it. I love Mary very much. She did not tell me herself but an angel told me. It may be hard for you to believe me but I wish you would because you are my best friend. You still will be my best man, won't you?

Bob: This is a bit much for me but, Joe, if you are convinced of this, I believe you. And yes, I will be your best man. You must really love that girl.

Joseph: Bob, I love her more than anything in the world and can you imagine. I am going to be the guardian father to the Son of God! Here, use my handkerchief.

For Christians, believing in the virgin birth is as important as believing that Jesus was crucified for our sins and that He arose from the dead. The character of Joseph is not discussed again in Matthew's gospel, probably because he was only a guardian parent but he was still a descendent of Abraham and David, men of God, who acted on faith. Jesus suffered tremendously but he had some great earth parents. Joseph might have died early in Jesus' life. But, Jesus worked with his father at least until age 12. Perhaps our Lord suffered the great loss of Joseph and had to bear a loss of someone He loved in order to fulfill a truly human existence. There is no mention of Joseph at the cross with Mary but I would think that he would have been there if he could have. What is really important is who is at the cross today.

Do you have a spiritual heritage? How so?

What kind of person was Joseph? Would we react the same way he did?

Is it difficult or easy to share the virgin birth story with others? Is it important that others believe in the virgin birth?

Day 3: Quarterback Qualifications

Scripture–Exodus, Chapters 1-3

Recalling Day 2, Exodus begins with a similar recap of heritage, starting with Joseph. Of course, this is a different Joseph and an entirely different setting but we find genuine parallels between the New Testament and the Old Testament. Our main character, Moses, was a descendent of the Levite tribe that would bear the priesthood of the Jewish faith. The name, Moses, means to be drawn out of the water. According to the decree of Pharaoh, Moses should have been executed at birth but the unexpected happened and a plan was put in place that would impact the lives of us all. Not only did Moses survive, he became a leader trained by circumstances.

Our leader could be compared to a quarterback of a team that had been building for 400 years in Egypt. He lived under the protection and guidance of a Pharaoh for 40 years; then he spent as many years working as a shepherd for his father-in-law. Finally, he spent the next 40 years leading people into an obscure desert wilderness. In God's timing, He would bring an 80 year old Moses forward to lead people from bondage to freedom.

Focus Scripture: Exodus 2:10

…and she named him Moses, and said, "because I drew him out of water."

Focus Scripture: Exodus 2:19

They answered, "An Egyptian rescued us from the shepherds. He even drew water for us and watered the flock."

Focus Scripture: Exodus 3:14

And God said to Moses, "I AM WHO I AM" and He said, "Thus you shall say to the sons of Israel. 'I Am has sent me to you.'"

I played a line position on a high school football team. We did not play well during my first year on the team. We lacked unity at first but in subsequent years we became more focused and our quarterback improved his passing and leadership skills. I believe that our coach improved, too. Moses was the quarterback of choice because of his experience and because the coach instilled the abilities into his man. God sees not only the play but the entire game; the entire season; the final outcome. Just as a quarterback needs confidence, so did Moses but God gave him authority when He laid down the qualifications as the Great I AM.

The parallel between a football team and a million people lead by Moses is valid to a point. Consider that God can use players from the opposition to move the ball toward the goal. The daughter of Pharaoh was not on God's team but she was an instrument of His divine will. The ultimate opposition, Pharaoh, was playing into the hands of God who knew that the oppression of the Hebrews would cause freedom. But, it is clear that God wants us to communicate with Him and state our feelings. He asks us to join in the cause and play our positions in unity under His leadership. We cannot know the outcome but we can be sure that we are trained for the moment, how ever young or old we may be.

Anyone who reads Exodus realizes that we won the game but the contest went into overtime when Moses tried to overrule the coach and call his own shot. Consequently, Moses played almost the entire game but was pulled in overtime and replaced by a different quarterback who took credit for leading the team across the goal line, into Israel. Our God wants our best in obedience and faithfulness and He will give us confidence in knowing that we are on the winning team.

Moses was about to lead people out of bondage and they were ready to accept his leadership. Ironically, these same people started to think about going back into bondage. They thought about the stability of Egypt and the annual floods of the Nile. They started to think that maybe they had it wrong. We do the same thing. We question our situation in life and have the audacity to question the leadership of God, thinking maybe He made some kind of mistake in our lives. Is not that thinking ridiculous? We must leave the bondage of sin that keeps us from being the kind of people that God intended us to be. We are called to make some decisions or "play calling" of our own.

What circumstances have impacted your life in a way that you can become a better leader?

In what ways does the death sentence to the baby boys born in Egypt parallel our spiritual condition? In what way does the rescue from the water parallel our spiritual condition?

How was the experience of Moses useful for his assignment?

To what extent do we control the playing field in our own lives?

How did Moses gain confidence as a leader, considering his background?

Day 4: Spare the goats

Scripture: Mark–Chapter 1

If two siblings have a quarrel and the parents demand an apology, the words, "I'm sorry" are often forced and insincere. They apologize only to get out of a situation without really expressing repentance for their behavior. Some times people apologize and then qualify the apology with a long explanation. "I'm sorry, but you know" is followed by an excuse that leaves one with the feeling that their apology was not really genuine, offered to restore peace rather than for the sake of reconciliation. Repenting extends an apology beyond a ritual phase and moves us into a mended condition of the heart.

Mark may have been the earliest gospel written and the first chapter reveals the life and purpose of Jesus. The new baptism was one of repentance without animal sacrifice, formerly the only means of obtaining reconciliation. Even with the perfect animal sacrifice, it is clear that a wealthy person could not follow the letter of Jewish law without really placing their hearts on the altar. Jesus started his ministry with this example of being baptized, showing all that there was a detail that needed to be addressed before embarking on His ministry.

Focus Scripture: Mark 1: 4, 5

And so John came, baptizing in the desert region and preaching a baptism of repentance for the forgiveness of sins. The whole Judean countryside and all the people of Jerusalem went out to him.

Focus Scripture: Mark 1:18

I baptized you with water; but He (Jesus) will baptize you with the Holy Spirit.

Focus Scripture: Mark 1:15

The time is fulfilled, and the kingdom of God is at hand: repent and believe in the gospel.

I am not sure that the people really knew (at the time of Jesus' first mentioning) what He meant when He said "believe in the gospel." Later on, they knew the spoken gospel and the power of the Holy Spirit. Years later (50 to 70 A.D.), the gospel of Mark was recorded. But the important point emphasized by both John the Baptist and Jesus was that a repentant heart was the pre-requisite for reconciliation and salvation. The Jewish people certainly understood the cleansing issue from Jewish law; now God's law was in their midst and a new era was about to commence.

The moment we think "please Lord, forgive me," we move back into that place where true harmony is restored. It is then that we have a clear image of the Captain taking hold of the rudder of our lives. He loves me before I ask for forgiveness but He does insist that I make the kind of apology that is total, sincere, and without excuses.

In verse 40 a leper came to Jesus and said "If you are willing, You can make me clean." What kind of cleansing did the Leper request? What kind of cleansing is Jesus asking of us?

Why was it important that Jesus undergo Baptism?

In the first chapter of Mark we find Jesus enlisting His disciples. Why do you suppose that these first disciples found it so easy to drop what they were doing and follow Jesus?

Are there any particular characteristics of Jesus that you see in this gospel that you would like to imitate?

Are there any other observations that strike you personally when you read this scripture?

Day 5: Get the goats

Scripture–Leviticus, Chapter 5 (Scan Chapters 1–4)

Someone told me that if you go to court for a traffic violation and the arresting officer does not show up, the ticket could be dismissed. I must confess that I tried this as I thought the violation was inflated but when I showed up at the court, my argument was weak and I looked pretty foolish. The judge said to me "that's it?" I was found guilty and had to pay the entire fine.

My excuse was that I was not familiar with the neighborhood but this was not grounds for violating the law (as the judge quickly pointed out). When we reflect on the requirements for atonement, as described in Leviticus, we are left with a feeling of gratitude that we do not have to go through the extremes of animal sacrifice or grain sacrifice. In Old Testament times, instead of paying money to the judge, we would be required to bring a lamb for sacrifice, slit the throat, and spread the blood in a specific manner over the altar.

Focus Scripture: Leviticus 5: 5, 6

So it shall be when he becomes guilty in one of these, that he shall confess that in which he has sinned. He shall also bring his guilt offering to the Lord for his sin which he has committed…

Focus Scripture: Leviticus 5: 17, 18

If a person sins and does what is forbidden in any of the Lord's commands, even though he does not know it, he is guilty and will be held responsible. He is to bring to the priest as a guilt offering a ram from the flock, one without defect and of the proper value. In this way the priest will make atonement for him for the wrong he has committed unintentionally, and he will be forgiven.

From the Leviticus line, came the priesthood which served as an intermediary between God and mankind. The law was very specific concerning the sacrifices and the means of atonement. The descriptions of animal sacrifice seem brutal and cult-like. If we read in a newspaper about a group of people who were sacrificing animals and paying close attention to the means of handling the organs of that animal, we would certainly not attribute it to a civilized, Jewish faith but what is described in Leviticus was the Law of the time.

We cannot understand everything about the way God thinks but we can realize one thing from the passage–God takes sin very seriously. The detail of sin is also serious to God, as he wants us to examine our own actions and see if we are sinning intentionally as well as unintentionally. He wants us to cut into the "tissue" of our daily lives and handle the sin in a way that is acceptable. For example, if we violate a traffic law and are caught, we may need to think about the priorities of our life and the safety of others rather than blame the arresting officer who pulled us over.

Thankfully, we do not have to do anything more than recognize our sin and change our direction, approaching God with the issue. God did the rest when He placed His Son on the altar. Can we possibly comprehend this kind of love and involvement in our lives? We can only fall down before the altar of sacrifice and weep with thanksgiving for His act of grace, knowing that He took our imperfections and supplied a perfect sacrifice.

Having said all this, there is something to be said about approaching God, even though we are not quite at a point of total submission. We may start off in prayer with a heart like a child who forces an apology to their sibling but if we talk to God long enough, our confession will become genuine. If we talk to Him even longer, we may find a means of reconciling differences with the person who we feel offended us. Of equal importance, we will become humbled and express sincere fault and God will render a sincere forgiveness.

Have you ever been angry because of something happened to you but realized later that you were the cause of the circumstance?

Looking ahead in Leviticus, we come upon a verse in Chapter 6 (vs.13) which says, "Fire shall be kept burning continually on the altar; it is not to go out." What might that mean to us as far as our lifetime walk with God?

Is guilt a good thing or a bad feeling? How so?

Are there "small" details in our lives that need correction?

Your personal observations, comparing yesterday's scripture instruction to Leviticus

Day 6: Who's the Son

Scripture–Luke Chapter 1

Sometimes we say, "I can't believe it, I just can't believe it!" On the eve of good news we exclaim these words, sometimes attaching them to luck. On some occasions we give God credit and express great gratitude. But sometimes we fall into a kind of intellectual sphere that is impermeable to the acceptance of God being ultimately in control over our destiny.

Chapter 1 of Luke's Gospel is long and packed with spiritual and literal truths that could impact us in many different ways. We find a priest, Zachariah, who had the privilege of burning incense in the temple of the Lord. He had a haunting and gnawing pain in his heart because he and his wife had no children and they were beyond the normal child bearing years. So he asked for a miracle, not really thinking that it would happen but he dreamed of maybe having a son who could continue his family.

Focus Scripture: Luke 1:3, 4

"...it seemed fitting for me...to write it out for you in consecutive order..."

Focus Scripture: Luke 1:15

"For he will be great in the site of the Lord, he will be filled with the Holy Spirit while yet in his mother's womb."

Earl Fashbaugh

Focus Scripture: Luke 1:41

"And it came about that when Elizabeth heard Mary's greeting, the baby leaped in her womb, and Elizabeth was filled with the Holy Spirit."

Doctor Luke, a physician, wrote this Gospel. At the time Doc Luke wrote this, there were other gospels circulating, mostly by word of mouth. There was a need to record a very systematic gospel and get all the facts on paper. Being a doctor, Luke knew all about the developmental process of a baby and he wanted to make sure that the reader would know the exact order and relationships of John the Baptist, Mary, Zachariah, Joseph, and Jesus.

Zachariah could not believe that his prayer was going to be answered. More importantly, he missed the implications of scripture being fulfilled as prophesied over 400 years ago about the child who would become John the Baptist. Mary was also in for a little surprise because six months after her cousin (Elizabeth) conceived she was going to also. The improbability of conception was even more so in Mary's case than Elizabeth but we see a great miracle on both ends – one where a woman had long since been marked as barren and unable to conceive and one where there was no earthly father involved. In his writing, Luke stretches out one hand to validate the past and the other hand to proclaim the glorious future.

We act surprised when prayer is answered. It is as if we send for something from a catalogue or order it online and then act surprised when it comes in the mail. Then, we try to take some credit for miracles that happen that have no logical explanation. We forget about the logic and divine will of God. It is then that our mouths should be latched shut and our heart thrown open as we hear with our hearts the great message of Love.

I was recently unemployed for a period of 14 months. I prayed for work as our reserves were getting skinny and my retirement funds would soon be used to pay the bills. "Please, God," I would ask. "Grant me a job. You know my needs. You know my extended family needs. Please give me work." He answered my prayer and gave me a perfect job, working with some excellent professionals. But, God waited to answer the prayer until everything was right and the order—the divine order of circumstances was fulfilled according to a blueprint.

Two women, one would conceive by the Holy Spirit and one with a baby filled with the Holy Spirit. One great plan and message of hope, knowing that our God hears prayer and He answers in the background, foreground, and in the future. We just have a difficult time seeing the perspective beyond our circumstances.

Are prayers being answered in your life in a way that you can't quite understand?

Chapter 1 in Luke is a long passage with many other noteworthy themes. What stands out to you, personally?

What great change occurred in Zachariah as illustrated in verse 67?

Zachariah could not name the baby after his own blood line. Instead, he named him, John, according to verse 63. Why do you think this is significant and what application does it have in our own sense of the future?

Is your blood line important to you? Why or why not?

Day 7: Sneeze in your sleeve

Scripture–Numbers 1-4 (scan); Numbers Chapter 5 (read)

Numbers. How many people live in North America? What is the birth rate? How much CO2 is liberated from a gallon of gasoline? What is the tallest building in New York City and how tall is it? These are all numbers. This fourth book of the Old Testament is about the Jewish people living between Egypt and their homeland. At first glance, it seems like an overdone emphasis of detail. In a sense, the author seems to be like Dr. Luke (Day 6) where both authors make painstaking efforts to get the facts recorded.

Numbers. How many times do you hear a phone number on a radio commercial? Sometimes you may hear the phone number quoted three times but many times, the advertiser will say it four times to make sure that it sticks in your brain. So, this book has repetition and lots of numbers to get a point across, to make sure that instructions are exact, and to make sure that the Laws are remembered.

Numbers. How many people left Egypt and how many entered the Promised Land? I do not know, but if a million left Egypt, a whole lot less made it across the Jordon due to disobedience and death. Could God be trying to tell an ancient people how to conduct themselves? Could God be telling a contemporary people, us, how we ought to behave?

Our children (two in number) were spared the experience of being left at a day care facility and were not infected as often as other children.

Nevertheless, they did get sick and often our entire family would come down with what ever the kids brought home from school. The Hebrews teach us a lesson on quarantine practices. It was the only way they could deal with diseases like leprosy. It would seem cruel, but isolation of diseased people was the only manner in which to keep the rest of the population healthy. Some of the isolation may have been unnecessary because it involved non-infectious conditions but God was emphasizing the point that physical or spiritual contamination needs to be avoided. We must wash our hands and minds, continuously.

Focus Scripture: Numbers 5:3, 4

"Send away male and female alike; send them outside the camp so they will not defile their camp, where I dwell among them." The Israelites did this; they sent them outside the camp. They did just as the Lord had instructed Moses.

Focus Scripture: Numbers 5:7

"Then he shall confess his sins which he has committed, and he shall make restitution in full for his wrong, and add to it one-fifth of it, and give it to him whom he has wronged."

Focus Scripture: Numbers 5:28

"But if the woman has not defiled herself and is clean, she will then be free and conceive children."

The scripture seems to suggest that restitution can be made for the tangible things of this world but to sin by adultery takes something away that cannot be replaced, trust and security. In a sense, a woman who leaves her husband in the Old Testament has contracted an incurable disease and she must be considered a curse to her community. A great change occurred in the New Testament, but unfaithfulness, whether forgiven or not is still grounds for divorce. One can confess sin but one cannot erase the consequences of sin. Only Jesus can help us through the times when we have completely blown it. Only Jesus can keep us clean so that we can remain within the camp of believers and not have to be quarantined from other believers.

One more focus Scripture is worth noting. It is found in Numbers 6, vs. 24-27, where the Lord instructed Moses and Aaron (his brother) how to bless the people:

"The Lord Bless you and keep you;
The Lord make his face shine upon you
And be gracious to you,
The Lord turn his face toward you and give you peace.

So they will put my name on the Israelites, and I will bless them." (Num. 6:24-27)

Numbers. What is your social security number? What is your driver's license number. How old are you? One funny bank commercial ends by asking, "what's in your wallet?" When it comes down to crossing the Jordon to be on the other side with the Lord, all the numbers of this life will be left behind. But for now, it makes a difference how we live our lives. May The Lord Bless you and keep you. May the Lord put His name on the Israelites—us.

Who causes us to sin?

Who causes us to repent?

Who can undo the consequences of sin?

Day 8: Believe it when I see it

Scripture–John 1:1–34

I was on a geology field trip in Colorado. After a lengthy discussion concerning the stratal relationships, one of the delegates on the trip said, "I would not have seen it unless I believed it," the inverse of our colloquial "I would not have believed it if I had not seen it." In essence the delegate on the trip was saying that we had already made some assumptions that lead to the conclusions about our observations. Sometimes we tend to look for ways to validate and verify what we already believe to be true. The point that the geologist was trying to make was that we were making assumptions, carried in on the backs of other assumptions. In essence, he was saying that we had extrapolated too far and that there was need to connect the observations differently or at least try to see if there could be another conclusion.

As Christians, we have run several extension cords to the truth of Jesus back over 2000 years. There is nothing wrong with that. After all, the truth does not change, whether it happened yesterday or five billion years ago. But, the book of John, written by John, is about setting everyone straight about where the power is coming from and he wants to make sure we plug in a single extension cord, connecting our faith to our personal beliefs.

When we read John's gospel we get the impression that he wanted to establish the truth about Jesus--who He was and what the world had. He also felt it important to convey who John the Baptist was and what his ministry was about. Our author, John, was an important eye-witness; he wanted the world to experience the life of Jesus and understand who was crucified and who He died for, and what we invest our hope in (today and forever). If we say, "I kind of believe in Jesus," we have a loose connection to the power source.

Focus Scripture: John 1:1-5

In the beginning was the Word, and the Word was with God, and the Word was God. He was with God in the beginning. Through him all things were made; without him nothing was made that has been made. In him was life, and that life was the light of men. The light shines in the darkness, but the darkness has not understood it.

Focus Scripture: John 1:12

Yet to all who received him, to those who believed in his name, he gave the right to become children of God—children born not of natural descent, nor of human decision or a husband's will, but born of God.

Focus Scripture: John 1: 30

"This is He on behalf of whom I said, 'after me comes a Man who has a higher rank than I, for He existed before me.'"

Focus Scripture: John 1:33-34

"The man on whom you see the Spirit come down and remain is he who will baptize with the Holy Spirit. And I have seen, and I testify that this is the Son of God."

Experts are sometimes brought in to testify in court. The attorney who calls the witness establishes the credentials of these people who may have expertise in forensics or DNA matching. The testimony often starts with a statement about where these individuals went to school and how long they studied in their given fields. But all these experts are nothing compared to someone who was at the scene of the crime or someone who was with the accused during the crime. If someone on the stand, under oath, says "I know this person is innocent because I was with him at the time of the crime," the jury must either decide that the accused is innocent or that the testimony is false. The other expert testimonies are usually secondary, compared to the eye-witness.

John quoted John the Baptist when he wrote, "this is the Son of God." We understand from the passage that the Holy Spirit descended on Jesus and also testified. John the Baptist made it clear that Jesus would be Baptizing with this same Holy Spirit. It is here that we see a picture of God, the Holy Spirit, and Jesus. But now, we can only "see" the Holy Spirit performing works through us that really know and bear witness of Jesus. We have, in essence, taken the words of John and affirmed them in our hearts. We have seen Jesus through the words that John took great care to record.

Do we believe because of what John wrote or do we believe because of what the Holy Spirit convinces us of? That is a bit of a mystery that circles back to our hearts as we take the stand in this world court. We are asked to testify why we believe that this Jesus was more than a man. We answer back in simple faith like a child, "Jesus loves me, this I know, for the Bible tells me so." If driven by the Holy Spirit, can there be a stronger argument?

Why do you believe what you do about God?

What might have been going on in the early church that John felt so strongly compelled to write this gospel, starting out so differently from the others?

The first chapter of John is a very long passage with many other striking testimonies. What stirs you the most?

How might we be compared to John the Baptist?

Day 9: Jack fell down, again

Scripture–Deuteronomy 1:1–2:7

Suppose I wrote, "Jack and Jill went up the hill to fetch a pail of water. Jack fell down and broke his crown and Jill came tumbling after." That would not tell you much beyond Jack having a mishap and Jill falling right behind him. But if I wrote, "Jack and Jill were having a glorious day as they walked up a steep but rocky hill to an artesian well where they would draw from a spring, fed by pure, cool water. Unfortunately, as they were descending Jack stepped on a loose stone and lost his footing. He tried to catch his balance but fell on his right shoulder and bounced off a granite boulder. His mind raced ahead of the situation wondering if he would ever see Jill again. She tried to catch up to Jack as he fell and she too succumbed to the unforgiving slope. Her blonde hair became matted with mud and a long branch ripped a gash in her ear as Jill's body rolled uncontrollably. They landed at the bottom of the slope, almost stunned to be alive and looked at each other. Jack spoke first and said, "where is the pail?"'

Ok, so the Old Testament seems repetitive and sometimes provides more detail than we might want to digest. Perhaps, all I want to hear is that Jack and Jill had an accident but both are doing fine. Deuteronomy goes into the heart of the story and gives us profound insights about the fall of Jack and what he did wrong (or what any of us have done wrong). The book tells a story about the people who longed for the Promised Land but trusted their own abilities and intuition. Still, God provided for His people in a part of the world that would not naturally sustain a million people. The Hebrew nation forgot who was providing for them, supernaturally.

Earl Fashbaugh

Focus Scripture: Deuteronomy 1:21

"See, the Lord your God has given you the land. Go up and take possession of it as the Lord, the God of your fathers, told you. Do not be afraid; do not be discouraged."

Focus Scripture: Deuteronomy 1:27

"You grumbled in your tents and said, 'because the Lord hates us, He has brought us out of the land of Egypt to deliver us into the hand of the Amorites to destroy us.'"

Focus Scripture: Deuteronomy 2:7

"For the Lord your God has blessed you in all that you have done; He has known your wanderings through this great wilderness. These forty years the Lord your God has been with you; you have not lacked a thing."

God protected the New Hebrew Nation even in the remoteness of the dessert. He provided water, food, shelter throughout the entire forty years and we stand afar in time and space and wonder how they could ever doubt the God that opened the corridors of the Red Sea and hung a curtain of water on either side of them. But I often ask for forgiveness when I realize that I have done the same thing when not trusting Him thoroughly when He has already brought me this far in a turbid world. It almost seems that we tend to think of Him less when we have more.

Every day offers a promised land, just as Caleb described it but we have to cross over and cease the territory of Godly lives and live beyond our circumstances, clinging to the crown, even when we have a great fall. We are challenged to the point of tears by financial burdens, death, chronic ailments, and disease. But, we mimic the wondering Hebrew Nation if we blame others for times that seem to lead us into spiritual wilderness. The God of Abraham, Isaac, and Jacob wants us to be courageous and not be discouraged by external influence.

When is the last time you felt like you were lead into a dessert without recourse?

Should we cease to plan (financially or otherwise) because we know that God will protect us?

What other observations can you make about the people involved in this portion of scripture?

We have taken snapshots of the first five books in the Old Testament and the four gospels of the New Testament. Even though the Old and New testaments are separated by a large span of time, in both cases we observe authors making sure that a point is driven into spiritual ground. Moses probably wrote most of the text in Genesis, Exodus, Leviticus, Numbers, and Deuteronomy (although someone else, perhaps Joshua wrote about his death). The message is sometimes repetitious but there appears to be a genuine desire to emphasize some key points in both the NT and OT. As we are only taking snapshots, it is hard to grapple with the connectivity of these writings. To do that requires more than casual reading but we can always cycle back and forth. There is great utility in seeing prophesies of the OT being referred to by Jesus and others in the NT. The more I read, pray, and talk with other Christians, the closer I draw to God and the more comfortable I become about the great Promised Land beyond the river of this life.

Day 10: On your mark, get set

Scripture–Acts 1: 1–26

Imagine being a disciple of Jesus after He ascended into heaven and contemplating the road ahead. There was work to be done but a nagging question confronted the apostles and other believers about the return of Jesus and His Kingdom on earth. Organizational issues had to be addressed now that the person of Jesus was gone. Instead of following Him around, there was a need for all of the apostles to take on leadership roles. They needed to meet but the temple was not available to these Christian Jews. Judas, who betrayed Jesus, needed to be replaced and basic necessities had to be addressed. But, the assembly of Christians, all 120 of them, had to wait until the Holy Spirit arrived and dwelled among the former fishermen and tax collectors. The situation could be compared to a bride waiting for the groom. But, when the Holy Spirit arrived, a new spark ignited a Faith that would glow stronger with time. The groom will come but only when He knows that the bride is ready.

If I have one glaring bad habit, it is to squander time. When I was in high school, I could not wait to get out; when I was in college, I had the same feelings. When I was in graduate school, I could hardly think of anything else than to be working. When we moved to one place, I could not wait to be transferred to another. Do you see the pattern? I still do this to a certain extent; even now I think about retirement to the point that it interferes with my job. This is not the way God wants us to deal with our situations and the early Christians of Jerusalem were an example of how we all aught to consider spending our time until God says to "go."

Focus Scripture: Acts 1:7-8 (Words of Jesus)

"It is not for you to know times or epochs which the Father has fixed by His own authority but you shall receive power when the Holy Spirit has come upon you; and you shall be My witnesses both in Jerusalem, and in all Judea and Samaria, and even to the remotest part of the earth."

Focus Scripture: Acts 1:11

"Men, of Galilee, why do you stand looking into the sky?"

Focus Scripture: Acts 1:14

"These all with one mind were continually devoting themselves to prayer, along with the women, and Mary the mother of Jesus, and with His brothers."

Instead of an end, it was a beginning. A baby was developing in the womb of Jerusalem and the baby's name would become the universal church of our Lord, Jesus Christ. The wait was not without purpose as people needed to get to know each other and barriers had to come down as people were taught to care for each other, regardless of their social status or gender. They needed to pray together, talk about the life of Jesus, contemplate the meaning of Jesus' parables, understand the fulfillment of scripture, and learn to share the message to others. Time was not wasted as they waited for the arrival of the Holy Spirit. Instead, they were all continually preparing themselves for the great Commission to share a belief that would forever change the world.

There are many more important points to glean from this message but a practical lesson on time management is glaring. We need to get on with the purpose of our lives as ordained and sanctioned by God. Then we can move on to the next step, what ever that may be.

What could you do today that would make you more prepared to face tomorrow?

How should we respond to other Christians who seem anxious about the future?

What are some things we do that interfere with our growth as Christians?

Judging from the Book of Luke and the Book of Acts, what kind of person was the author?

Record other observations that you think are important about the first church.

Day 11: Go on the green light

Scripture - Joshua 1:1-18

There are no shortages of people or businesses that claim to have the secrets to success. The Wall Street Journal promises a financial advantage if you read their newspaper. The automobile manufactures suggest that a new car will result in happiness and a relationship. The exercise industry promises six pack abdominal muscles. Cosmetic and shampoo companies surely claim the means of achieving incredible beauty. And if all else fails, the Insurance companies will help you make plans for a successful retirement, if not for you, certainly for your spouse. We are hosed every day with guarantees; we sort through all the noise and look for the substance in this life.

If the Book of Acts, chapter 1 (Day 10 Snapshot) was about waiting on God and preparing, Joshua is a Book that guarantees success in putting faith in motion. It was necessary for the early Christians of Acts to wait in Jerusalem and meet together and pray regularly until the Holy Spirit was with them, but after that, the message was to put the vehicle in gear and get moving.

Focus Scripture: Joshua 1:7

Only be strong and very courageous: be careful to do according to all the law which Moses My servant commanded you; do not turn from it to the right or to the left, so that you may have success wherever you go.

Focus Scripture: Joshua 1:9

"Have I not commanded you? Be strong and courageous!" Do not tremble or be dismayed, for the Lord your God is with you wherever you go.

Focus Scripture: Joshua 1:16

Then they answered Joshua, "Whatever you have commanded us we will do, and wherever you send us we will go."

One time I failed a behind the wheel driver's test. How? I came to a stop light, looked both ways, and then proceeded to make a left turn. I was so concerned that the officer would note that I was looking both ways that I failed to honor a red light. If you break a law, the officer explained after my examination, you fail the test. My fear caused my failure. If I had relaxed and just obeyed the simple law, I would have scored perfectly on the drivers test. So it is with God's instruction to us to obey the Commandments of God and then proceed with courage.

The nation Israel was about to cross the Jordan River and a new leader carried a mandate directly from God. Some people may have been frightened. They were not, after all, a warring nation; they were nomads who were to occupy a land promised to their ancestor, Abraham. But God sent a time-tested guarantee that is valid today. We must constantly rely on His Word and His guidance and rest assured that there is no mistake where God wants us to be or what God wants us to do. We have freedom within sphere of His proclamation that "God is with you wherever you go" (Joshua 1:9).

Crossing the Jordan River during Biblical times took courage. The Hebrews would descend one steep bank and walk through (what they thought) would be deep, rushing water; then they would ascend the other western bank of the river. But Joshua told the people to keep their eyes out for the Ark of the Covenant and follow where it was carried. Just as the generation crossed the Red Sea, the followers crossed on dry land into the safety of their new (but promised) land. Note, they kept their eyes on the Promise of God and His word—they then were able to overcome all fear.

Have you ever done something that you regretted later on and wished you could wind back the clock?

Have you ever failed to do something that you realized you should have?

Given the two questions above, how do we proceed in this life?

If we obey the commandments of God, is it possible to make mistakes? Is it possible that we are somewhere physically or spiritually that we should not be if God has set a plan in motion?

Think about some of the concerns of the new nation, Israel, and compare them to what concerns you may have at this moment in your life.

Record any snapshots of your own about the passage.

Day 12: Stop on the red light

Scripture–Romans 1: 1–32

My brother was bow hunting one time and he set a strung bow in the back seat of the car. The local game warden spotted the bow and issued a citation for having a strung bow outside of a case (inside a motorized vehicle). My brother, Jack, made light of the situation and said he did not know that this was a violation of Minnesota law. The game warden simply informed him "if you want to hunt, you better know the regulations." Jack went home and told Dad what had happened and my father was angry. He was not angry at my brother but he was irritated with the law and a game warden that would enforce such a "ridiculous" regulation. The game warden was the father of one of my good friends so I started to resent anyone who my father resented, all this over a law that did not seem to have any purpose. Would it not be more reasonable for the warden to explain the law and then tell Jack not to do it again?

Focus Scripture: Romans 1:5, 6

Through him and for his name's sake, we received grace and apostleship to call people from among all the Gentiles to the obedience that comes from faith. And you also are among those who are called to belong to Jesus Christ.

Focus Scripture: Romans 1:20

For since the creation of the world His invisible attributes, His eternal power and divine nature, have been clearly seen, being understood through what was been made, so that they are without excuse.

Focus Scripture: Romans 1:32

"...and, although they know the ordinance of God, that those who practice such things are worthy of death, they not only do the same, but also give hearty approval to those who practice them."

If there were one book in the Bible that dealt with the great theological questions of all ages, it is Romans and Chapter 1 deals with accountability. Our author, Paul, suggests an element of innocence in not knowing the law but he also talks about severe punishment for those who know the Law of God and yet go about violating and promoting others to do the same thing.

The first Christians of Rome and Greece were confronted with a question of guilt and the scholars of that time were drilling them for answers. Does this sound familiar? Has anyone ever asked you, "How could a loving God condemn others for not believing?" Paul's response to that would be that we start out in a condemned state but are only accountable for what we know to be true. If that were the end of the story, we should want to know nothing about Christ and just stare up at the stars and thank God for all creation. But then, we would not have provisions for dealing with our sinful nature. So it goes, we make up human laws and when we study cultures that have not been subject to Biblical knowledge, we see that they adopt similar regulations about how to conduct themselves. These man-made laws are sometimes contrary to Bible teaching but all cultures establish taboos. Sometime, tribal laws are aligned perfectly with God's regulations. All "primitive" people have a sense of God and they call Him by different names. Those that claim to be atheists had to "un-learn" their belief in God. Of course, they will usually deny ever believing in God in the first place.

So, is the tribe in South America that has always lived in isolation responsible for not knowing about Jesus? No, but if they are told by missionaries that there is a plan for them and a Law of the Heart that is available, and if they reject this law, then they are condemned. But Paul is not saying that ignorance is best. He is simply introducing the concept of Grace that is expanded in subsequent chapters.

Should my brother have been fined? Yes. He should have read the regulations spelled out in a book issued with every hunting license. If the game warden were God, he could know that Jack was telling the truth about being unaware that the law was being broken. A game warden God would also know that Jack was not out to use the bow and arrow maliciously. However, the human game warden, or any other officer of the law, simply enforces the regulations. In this case the purpose of the regulation was so that people would not stop their car and shoot at a deer or anything else, at any time of the day. The law reduces the level of poaching in Minnesota and is probably a good regulation. So, we see that laws have purpose, even when we do not fully understand the intent of the statute and that would apply to God's regulations as well.

Our reaction to law can be one of acceptance and appreciation, rage, or intentional rejection. As far as God's Law, once we know the love of God, we want to love His Law and be obedient. Unfortunately, we choose not to obey God, continuously. When we fail to obey we separate ourselves from God and that separation would be eternal if not for ongoing, saving Grace. Our snapshot is restricted to the first chapter but to delve deeper into the subject of grace would require digestion of the first 9 chapters of Paul's epistle to the Romans.

Every verse in Romans, Chapter 1 could be a Focus Scripture. If you were writing this page, what particular verse would you want to emphasize and why?

If you have ever been arrested for any violation, what phases of reaction did you endure and how might these reactions be compared to our violation of God's Law?

When does Grace occur?

Day 13: Just a little rust

Scripture – Judges: Chapters 1 and 2

The second car I owned was a 1957 Chrysler with a push-button automatic. It was a fun car to drive, especially since gas was about 30 cents a gallon. The car was white and had modest fins and at least two white-wall tires. But it had developed a little problem with rust as many Minnesota cars do. I asked some high school friends of mine how I might fix the rust and most said that I had to sand all the rust off, put bondo body filler in the holes, sand it, put a coat of primer on, sand it with a fine grade paper, and then apply at least one coat of the recommended manufacturer's paint. This all seemed reasonable but I did not have that kind of patience so I sanded the car pretty thoroughly, put fiberglass in the holes and found an off-white shade of paint at the local hardware store. The car did not look too bad after that effort, especially just after sundown, so I was good to go and ready to enjoy a summer of cruising. Four months later the car looked as bad, or worse than when I first made a lame attempt to restore it. The tell-tale rust was bleeding through the bad paint job. I had not completely followed instructions from the guys who knew that the repair required complete removal of the rust, specific materials, and the correct finishing. The nation Israel was given a good car that needed restoration but they did the same thing I did and tried to take short cuts in preparing the land for occupancy.

Focus Scripture: Judges 1:21

"...But the sons of Benjamin did not drive out the Jebusites who lived in Jerusalem; so the Jebusites have lived with the sons of Benjamin in Jerusalem to this day."

Focus Scripture: Judges 2:2-3

"'...you shall make not a covenant with the inhabitants of this land; you shall tear down their altars.' But you have not obeyed Me; what is this you have done? Therefore, I also said, 'I will not drive them out before you; but they shall become as thorns in your sides, and their gods shall be a snare to you.'"

Focus Scripture: Judges 2:11-12

"Then the sons of Israel did evil in the sight of the Lord, and served the Baals, and they forsook the Lord the God of their fathers..."

The land west of the Jordon was occupied by a population that worshipped a wide variety of images in an effort to appease that inward need for God. The Canaanites, Jebusites, and others looked to their own conscience to understand God; but they desired to worship something or someone other than the One God. The Hebrews knew better. Their God had performed miracle upon miracle so that they could cross into this Promised Land and become a strong nation.

However, in the process of conquering the territory, the "rust" was not completely removed from the land. In fact, after time, the Hebrews decided they liked the diversity of gods. They fell into their own snare as God had warned and the consequence was a very inconsistent life style that dishonored God and lead to corruption of the chosen people.

God wants us to live Holy Lives and free from the garbage of this world. However, our cars do not sit in the garage. We are subject to the corrosive elements of a secular society and must continuously purge our minds and hearts of the rust that brings about destruction and unhappiness. Progressive erosion and corrosion of our character causes us to take on a fake and covered up appearance to the rest of the world and our attempt to be disciples is severely damaged from the inside out, just like the car I tried to fix. We can hide the rust and corrosion for a while but it will eventually show through.

According to the scripture reading, how did God deal with behavior of the Israelites?

Does He deal with us in a similar fashion when we stray from His will?

What other metaphors can we draw from the rusty car analogy? Alternatively, write down your own analogy.

Why do we feel miserable when we disobey God?

Your snapshot of the scripture:

Day 14: Quite a bit of rust

Scripture–1 Corinthians, Chapter 1

Referencing Day 13, I am not especially proud about the way I took care of my car, but I am even more ashamed of the life I formerly lead. I am occasionally reminded by a very good friend of mine that I drove my car right by him on some pretty cold mornings, rather than giving him a ride to school. First, let me tell you something about my friend, John. He was always a little big for his age and came from a family that did not have abundant financial resources. Some kids thought he looked a little nerdish with his thick plastic glasses but he was very smart and a harder worker in school. He never received a grade lower than an A- from grade school to graduation and went on to attend MIT where he also did very well.

I passed John up on those cold mornings because I wanted to pick up girls and have them for my own amusement while driving off to school. I wanted to look cool and not be associated with the very friend that I hung out with during most of my childhood. John has forgiven me and we continue to be good friends but I cannot help but to be reminded of the distorted values that I had and how I could have treasured more the presence of my wise and kind friend than the image of being cool. In Paul's time, Corinth was the learning and trade center of the world. This was the place to be, where philosophy flourished, cutting edge medicine was practiced, and there was plenty of sex. One does not have to wonder long if there has ever been a place like Corinth. It is the life of the United States with all sorts of videos making fun of the faithful and flaunting the ungodly.

Focus Scripture: 1 Corinthians 1:20

Where is the wise man? Where is the scribe? Where is the debater of this age? Has not God made foolish the wisdom of this world?

Focus Scripture: 1 Corinthians 1:27

But God has chosen the foolish things of the world to shame the wise, and God has chosen the weak things of the world to shame the things which are strong.

Focus Scripture: 1 Corinthians 1:31

"...that, just as it is written, 'let him who boasts, boast in the Lord.'"

Paul's letter suggests that there were specific instances where the wise people of this world tried to claim a true and deeper understanding than the rest of the population. The messages of Day 13 and 14 have similar themes. Both imply that cleansing must be from the inside out. Paul's letter to the church of Corinth suggests that there is only one person who can cleanse us: Jesus.

I was a Christian back in high school when I drove my rusted out 57 Chrysler right past my good friend. That would seem hard to believe but we all drive right by our brothers and sisters in the Lord on a daily basis because we think of ourselves before others. Paul clearly wanted us to cling to unity and true happiness through Christ rather than exchanging the truth for a lie (Romans 1:25).

My friend, John is eternal but the fading moment of my youth was temporary. When we fix our lives temporarily, we reap temporary happiness and the consequences are depressing. When we fix things permanently, we reap the consequences of living a complete and meaningful life.

Why did the people of Corinth try to align themselves with particular church leaders?

What are some examples of "world wisdom" that is actually foolishness to the world?

Day 15: Hey, we're related

Scripture: Ruth 1:1 – 4:22 (entire book)

When we look at life from the large end of binoculars, it is very small; that is the way we sometimes see our purpose. As we mature, life is seen from the small end of the oculars and it has depth and purpose. When I was an undergraduate at Eau Claire, Wisconsin, I suddenly decided that I needed to attend a different college so that I could get a degree in education as well as geology. On arrival and after reviewing my transcript with the head of the department, I was told that some of my previous course work would have to be repeated in order to fulfill their requirements. I was crushed as I could only see through the large end of the binoculars and the extra half year in school seemed unbearable. It was at UMD that I met my wife, Susan. As I write these words, I reflect back on 34 wonderful years of marriage, a great career, and two great kids who know Jesus as Lord. Now I am looking through the right end of the binoculars.

Ruth is a book that presents a story of two women, Mother and daughter-in-law, who must deal with a very grim situation but the mother, Naomi, always believed that she would see life through the large end of the binoculars. She believed this, even though she lost her husband and two sons. It must have been difficult for Naomi to lose her husband at such a young age but the big picture of the book of Ruth reveals something very wonderful in the last three verses of the book.

The paradox of Ruth requires several "snapshots" to absorb all of this scripture. Ultimately, the reader understands that the lineage of Jesus' guardian father, Joseph, goes back to the offspring of Ruth. We see a plan that was established long before Naomi or Ruth were born. We see a grand picture of Gentiles being spliced back into the lineage of God's people.

Focus Scripture: Ruth 4:14

And the women said unto Naomi, "blessed be the Lord, who hath not left thee this day without a kinsman, that his name may be famous in Israel."

Focus Scripture: Ruth 4:17

And the women, her neighbors, gave him a name, saying, "there is a son born to Naomi" and they called his name Obed: he is the father of Jesse, the father of David.

Focus Scripture: Ruth 4:22

And Obed begot Jesse, and Jesse begot David.

Both Naomi's sons died and she was widowed. But, her daughter-in-law, Ruth married and gave birth to a son--a very significant son, Obed. This baby boy was a forefather to David. Note that the lineage of David actually includes a half-Moabite, Ruth. The Moabites were not God fearing Jews. They were idol worshippers, completely cut off from God's people. Joseph, the earthly guardian of Jesus was partly a descendent of a group of people that were not supposed to be blessed. God's plans do not often match our intuition. More importantly, we see a plan in the binoculars that calls for us, non-Jewish people to become part of the plan for salvation.

The loving woman, Ruth, decided to become a Godly woman after the example of Naomi. What should have happened did not. Instead of Ruth staying in her homeland, she went with Naomi after her husband died. Ruth would have been content to be a slave in order to provide for her mother-in-law. This kind of humble attitude exemplifies the lovingness which is the true lineage of Christ. Instead of "blood-lines" we experience the benefits of a "love-line." This kind of family tree extends back to the creation of matter where nothing seen or unseen is made without God's time transcending love.

In your own life, did you ever experience an event that seemed impossible or even tragic, and yet this turned out to be a good thing?

How can we understand God's commandment to Joshua to completely destroy the Moabites and yet know that the house of Jesse would include this line of heritage?

Do we always see the outcome of our lives? Do we ever see the outcome of our lives and how we impact others?

Day 16: The lapidary process

Scripture – II Corinthians 1: 1-24

We gave our daughter a rock tumbler for Christmas. It was delightful to see her open the box and see the colorful canister and some rough rock and mineral samples that were included with the kit. We were all somewhat surprised to read the instructions that called for the rocks to be tumbled for eight straight days. For two days the samples tumbled with the carbide grit and we could not help but to check the canister and see if any progress had been made. The rocks did not look much different from when we first entered them in the tumbler. It was going to take the full eight days, as described in the directions.

Focus Scripture II Corinthians 1: 3, 4

Praise be to God and Father of our Lord Jesus Christ, the Father of compassion and the God of all comfort, who comforts us in all our troubles, so that we can comfort those in any trouble with comfort we ourselves have received from God.

Focus Scripture: II Corinthians 1:6

"But if we are afflicted, it is for your comfort and salvation; or if we are comforted, it is for your comfort, which is effective in the patient enduring of the same suffering which we also suffer..."

Focus Scripture: II Corinthians 1:20

> For as many as may be the promises of God, in Him they are yes; wherefore also by Him is our Amen to the glory of God through us.

One thing we can count on is affliction. We will go through the growing pains of adolescence, the mid-age crisis, and depression that will try to overcome us after our bodies have "tumbled" for about 70 years. But, the entire time that we are bumping into other "rocks" and even abrading each other, we become a little more polished in the process. The promises of God are that He controls the lapidary of this world and He is making and molding us through multiple sources, including other believers.

After eight days in the tumbler my daughter and I were delighted to see what the painstaking and noisy process had done. Our assortment of rocks had become uniquely beautiful after enduring the continuous motion in black, sooty looking grit and water. The grit is like the afflictions of life while the water can be compared to the enduring promise of God's presence in our lives.

The ultimate affliction was endured for us in the perfect life of Jesus and in His violent death on the cross, insuring that the tumbler would keep turning until we are ready to come out of this world and stand before the maker of the gemstones. If the message is repetitious, then so is the tumbler that changes us.

The promises of God are very directive and steadfast. If we stay the course of looking to Him for guidance through all sorts of trials in our life, we will draw closer. When we draw closer, the hard edges are taken off and the agate within starts to come out. Just as there are no two agates that are alike, neither are there two people the same that go through the lapidary process in this wonderful preamble of life.

Can you think of others who have endured for your benefit and well being and how can they be compared to the provisions of God?

As you think about the afflictions of Naomi (Day 15), was she able to see how the affliction would turn out?

In Paul's letter to the Corinthians, what kind of afflictions may have been endured by the disciples?

Provide an example of how affliction has had a positive effect in your life.

Can you think of anyone that you should pray about who may be enduring great affliction at this moment?

What are the promises of God?

Select a completely different verse from Chapter 1 and describe why you think that this is especially meaningful to you.

Day 17: A robe of love

Scripture – 1 Samuel 1:1 to 2:21

My mother has been gone for over 20 years now and not long ago my wife's Mom passed away. There is something very special about a mother's love; the more loving a mother, the more loving the children. It is no surprise that our adult children are very compassionate people. Mothers get angry but Moms always forgive and they give of themselves until they rest at night, only to rise the next day and repeat their loving ways. Years later we reflect back on our mothers and realize how much they did for us: everything from holiday costumes to the quiet talk about our relationships with others. Moms seem to love us even when they are not with us. This is the kind of woman Hannah was with great unconditional love for Samuel but even greater love for God. She fully realized after years without children that her son was truly a gift from God. She further vowed that her son would be dedicated to the work of the Lord.

Focus Scripture: 1 Samuel 1:10

"…O Lord Almighty, if you will only look upon your servant's misery and remember me, and not forget your servant but give her a son, then I will give him to the Lord…"

Focus Scripture: 1 Samuel 1:19, 20

> Early the next morning they arose and worshiped before the Lord and then went back to their home at Ramah. Elkanah lay with Hannah his wife, and the Lord remembered her. So in the course of time Hannah conceived and gave birth to a son. She named him Samuel, saying, "because I asked the Lord for him."

Focus Scripture: 1 Samuel 1:27, 28

> "'For this boy I prayed, and the Lord has given me my petition which I asked of Him. So I have also dedicated him to the Lord; as long as he lives he is dedicated to the Lord." And he worshiped the Lord there."'

Focus Scripture: 1 Samuel 2:19

> "And his mother would make him a little robe and bring it to him from year to year when she would come up with her husband to offer the yearly sacrifice."

It is hard to imagine what feelings pierced this woman's heart as she made a robe for her son every year. At that single day of the year she presented him with a gift. Her love was not the kind of selfish type that some parents may have. Rather, this was the kind of love that only comes from God. Perhaps she hugged him and he hugged her, thinking how nice it was but Samuel knew he had a higher calling for the Lord. He never forgot those moments while he stood beaming up at his mother from his new robe.

The land of Judah was transformed from a system of judges to a system of kings, and Samuel had the roll of using his gift of discernment and prophesy to know who would receive the blessing of leading their young country. He would bless the new king with a simple word and this word came from the loving heart of his mother. Again, the scripture points to a kinship of love as the house of David would be the ultimate source of God's plan through Jesus Christ.

What similarities and differences are there when we "dedicate" our infant children to the Lord?

Do we have a tendency to commit something or someone to the Lord and then withdraw?

Day 18: A wedge in the oak

Scripture – Galatians 1:1 to 2:10

When I was growing up, there were three things that Dad, my brother (Jack), and I did, together. We would go water skiing, fishing, or work on the wood pile. It turns out that working on the wood pile was the most unifying activity and it was kind of a "guy thing" that allowed us to use our muscles and ingenuity to put up next years supply of wood. We would usually find an oak that had blown over and start the wonderful process of cutting the large chunks of wood, hauling them away in our Ford Ranchero, dumping them in a large pile for initial splitting, and then split them again for the drying pile. Oak has kind of a pungent smell when it is green but it is the best wood for a hot, long-lasting fire. So when we stared into the fire on those cold Minnesota nights, we would reflect on where the wood came from, perhaps the day we gathered it, and maybe about the times we split it for drying.

Splitting oak can be a very challenging process, especially if the logs have knots in them. The wood is dense and hard to the point that it is difficult to imagine that a sturdy tree could ever be reduced to fire wood. It often requires a small wedge to initiate a crack, followed by a larger wedge, and then the wonderful rhythmic pounding of the wedge in order to get the log to finally fall apart. After the initial split, the subsequent splitting is not as difficult. Eventually a chunk of oak, starting at nearly 5 feet in diameter, becomes a good basket of dry wood.

The church was planted as a sturdy oak tree, founded in the gospel. But, soon after the church of Galatia was founded there was diversity never seen before in a gathering of believers, and this diversity sometimes was like a small wedge placed in a large piece of oak. Jews and gentiles were bringing their own ideas to church. Devout Jews were telling new converts how to conduct themselves while the Gentile converts were arguing about whose instruction they should follow. In other regions, Christians were circulating written material that they claimed to be the true gospel and inevitably, people were hearing the word but were confused and started to drift away. Instead of a strong piece of oak, the wedge of jealously, false wisdom, cultural differences, and many others were working at splitting up the early church.

Focus Scripture: Galatians 1:8

Am I now trying to win the approval of men, or of God? Or am I trying to please men? If I were still trying to please men, I would not be a servant of Christ.

Focus Scripture: Galatians 2:5

But we did not yield in subjection to them for even an hour, so that the truth of the gospel might remain with you.

Focus Scripture: Galatians 2:8

For God, who was at work in the ministry of Peter as an apostle to the Jews, was also at work in my ministry as an apostle to the Gentiles.

Paul writes as an authority. Even though he never saw Jesus when He was in the flesh, Paul was given apostleship because of His encounter with Christ on the road to Damascus. He carried the true, unblemished gospel of Jesus and had to swing his sword of truth so that others would not swing their axe to split the church. Paul knew that the arguments about circumcision, baptism, and outside doctrine were alienating people. The wedge had to be stopped and this letter to the church of Galatia was intended to call people together like a gnarly oak, able to stave off the satanic wedges that are with us even today…especially today.

I visited a church one time in New Orleans that had just fired their pastor. I had my offering ready to place in the basket when someone got up and said, "what happened to our pastor?" From there, a deluge of bitterness flowed from the congregation, and instead of a message of unity, I heard a message of hatred. There was not going to be a message from the pulpit that day. As I had never been there before, I quietly slid out the side isle, gave my offering to one of the ushers, and left. I am a Christian so there was no spiritual damage done to me, but I had to pray for those in the church that may have not made a full commitment to Christ. Perhaps that would be the day that a wedge would forever separate some people from a church experience. At the very least, it was a low point in that congregation's history when several left the fellowship.

Paul's letter to the Galatians shows that there was division in the early church as there is today; this letter just emphasizes that differences will occur. We are challenged to respond out of love and not out of self-serving interests. When leadership becomes rigid for the sake of tradition, then a wedge can be placed in the heart of a congregation. That is not to say that firm principles and sound doctrine can be manipulated. Rather, we must deal with infiltration of new ideas by testing them with the Carpenter's Level—the Word of God.

What causes differences between people?

We took a snapshot at one problem in the church of Galatia. What other observations do you make from this portion of scripture?

71

Paul writes, "But even if we or an angel from heaven should preach a gospel other than the one we preached to you, let him forever be condemned!" (Gal. 1:8). In the context of doctrinal differences, what does Paul mean?

How should we deal with differences in opinions of other Christians or non-Christians?

Day 19: You the man

Scripture - II Samuel: 1: 1-27

In our efforts to make quick snapshots at the beginning of the books in the Bible we skip over significant history. Point in case, we did not read about the rise of Saul, his anointing as King and his attempts to kill David. More importantly, we did not delve into the anointing process that would make Saul the first monarch of Judah. Samuel anointed Saul; then David—after Saul eventually fell from the grace of God's blessings. We take a quick snapshot that records a great friendship between David and Saul's son, Jonathan. This friendship emphatically inspires steadfast devotion between people.

When we think back on our "Best Man" or the "Maid of Honor" at our own weddings, it is likely that we would not chose that same person if we were married (or re-married) today. Just ten years after marriage, friendships change; our interests and family situations change. We tend to draw near to different people during different times in our lives. Usually, however, we think of a few people that have such significance in our lives that we classify them as "golden friends." They are the kind of friends that we care very much about. We care for their spouses and their children and they can become closer than blood relations. They are the kind of friends who are welcome at any time of the day and they feel the same thing about us. My wife and I have some of these kinds of friends and if they die before we do, we will certainly grieve the loss and we will feel a huge void in our hearts. They are the gem quality friends of our lifetime.

Focus Scripture: II Samuel 1: 11, 12

> Then David and all the men with him took hold of their clothes and tore them. They mourned and wept and fasted till evening for Saul and his son Jonathan, and for the army of the Lord and the house of Israel, because they had fallen by the sword.

Focus Scripture: II Samuel 1:14

> "Then David said to him, 'How is it you were not afraid to stretch out your hand to destroy the Lord's anointed?'"

Focus Scripture: II Samuel 1:26

> "I am distressed for you my brother Jonathan; you have been very pleasant to me. Your love to me was more wonderful than the love of women."

A young man informed David that he helped end the life of King Saul, as he was apparently fatally wounded. Perhaps the soldier thought that there would be a reward. Instead, he was sentenced to death. David made it clear that what was declared of God could not be reversed, except by God himself. Amazingly, Saul would have killed David if he could have because the spirit of guilt, jealousy, and paranoia had taken over the leader's heart. But, David's heart was directed toward God and his fallen friend, Jonathan.

Friendships like David and Jonathan's are precious and we need to take care of those rare friendships when they come along in this life. Moreover, we should try to encourage those friendships that germinate between believers in our Lord Jesus. From such relationships we can share our hurts and frustrations, sometimes better than we can with our own spouse. Our best friends become sounding devises in a world where decisions require careful consideration.

David declared that this kind of friend is more wonderful than the love of women. There is nothing weird about this declaration. I can certainly think of a few items that I can talk about with male friends that I would not feel comfortable sharing with my wife. We find a system of accountability built into this kind of relationship where one friend cares for another and keeps them in constant earshot.

David initially had two wives but soon after becoming King, he acquired more wives and concubines. More is not always better, especially when the wives were not soul mates. His friend, Jonathan, was a fellow who genuinely cared about David's happiness and well being. Although, Jonathan would have been heir to the throne, he was killed. If a friend along the lines of Jonathan had been available to David, is it possible that David would have not fallen into a sinful trap during his reign as king? Perhaps that is not a fair question because the fall of Saul and his household was necessary in order for David to become king. The point of discussion is that friends can be a means of staying on course in our walk with God.

Who are your closest friends; what have you done lately to nurture that friendship?

Why is it important that we have Christian friends?

Your observations about this passage:

Day 20: Stuck in the gully

Scripture – Ephesians 1: 1-23

I was a new employee, working on a drilling project near Douglas, Wyoming. We were drilling a hole to test for uranium in sands at about 1500 feet beneath the surface. In the adjacent section, a competitor was conducting a similar drilling program but we were not sure if they were targeting the same interval. I thought it would be commendable if I could find out this information so decided to take some time to drive my pickup truck into the adjacent property and investigate their drilling results. A narrow gully separated the two drilling sites but I thought my four-wheel drive vehicle could easily negotiate the poorly defined trail. I thought wrong. Both axles hung, and the truck was no longer supported by my wheels making it necessary to jack the vehicle up and put rocks under the tires. Even my winch proved to be useless when I tried to hook it on a small tree. There were few good size rocks available so I used four sacks of concrete that were in the back of the truck. However, when I put the truck in reverse and gave it gas, the wheels ripped open the bags and rendered my truck in dry concrete mix. No problem, except that it was starting to rain so that either enough rain would fall to totally flood the gully or enough would fall to get the concrete wet and cement my company truck in the valley. I prayed for help and wisdom.

Our snapshot of Paul's letter to the Ephesians emphasizes the importance of relying on God continuously in all we do instead of on our own will and abilities. When we depend on our own intellect without the power of the

Holy Spirit, we become like a hung up, four wheel drive vehicle. This is true whether we are housekeepers or brain surgeons. The Greek philosophers of Jesus time emphasized looking to our intellect for problem solving, but the message of Christ says that we need to look for supernatural wisdom in all aspects of life.

Focus Scripture: Ephesians 1:5

"He predestined us to adoption as sons through Jesus Christ to Himself, according to the kind intentions of His will."

Focus Scripture: Ephesians 1:18

"I pray that the eyes of your heart may be enlightened, so that you may know what is the hope of His calling, what are the riches of the glory of His inheritance in the saints…"

Focus Scripture: Ephesians 1: 21

"…far above all rule and authority and power and dominion, and every name that is named, not only in this age, but also in the one to come."

Adopted sons and daughters of Christ, we are brought under the wings of God. Our Lord builds in us a feeling of comfort and confidence, not of our selves but in what He can do with us. When I was stuck in the valley with my truck, a long ways from my drilling project, I was no longer a smart, young geologist who could conquer. I was a meek, foolish, and humiliated young man who needed to get help. The solution was to walk to the rancher's house, confess my fault, ask for forgiveness and help in getting out of the valley…..before the concrete set up.

How does the predestination of God relate to your calling?

Reflecting back on the anointing of David as King (Day 19), was His calling predestined? Were the fall of King Saul and the nature of his death predestined?

When evil things happen to us, are they predestined, a result of our actions, or part of a grander plan that we cannot see?

Note: the above questions are not intended to confuse the personal meaning of scripture but to stimulate thoughts about God's wisdom as opposed to ours. It cannot be emphasized enough that the Bible was written for us by those inspired by God so the words that we read take on very personal meaning. That is not to say that there is unlimited latitude in our interpretation of the Word. But, we must always be plugged in by confessing our sin and recognize a situation where we have driven the vehicles of our lives into a valley. In times of hopelessness, we can find hope by walking back to the "Rancher" and asking for help.

Do you see any similarities of the early church and the one we know today?

What portion of this passage seems especially applicable to you and why?

Day 21: To be a king

Scripture – 1 Kings 1:1-2:9

Look at this letter written by Abraham Lincoln.

Executive Mansion
Washington, December 23, 1862.

Dear Fanny
It is with deep grief that I learn of the death of your kind and brave
Father; and, especially, that it is affecting your young heart beyond
what is common in such cases. In this sad world of ours, sorrow comes
to all; and, to the young, it comes with bitterest agony, because it takes
them unawares. The older have learned to ever expect it. I am anxious
to afford some alleviation of your present distress. Perfect relief is
not possible, except with time. You can not now realize that you will
ever feel better. Is not this so? And yet it is a mistake. You are sure
to be happy again. To know this, which is certainly true, will make
you some less miserable now. I have had experience enough to know
what I say; and you need only to believe it, to feel better at once. The
memory of your dear Father, instead of an agony, will yet be a sad
sweet feeling in your heart; of a purer and holier sort than you have
known before.

Please present my kind regards to your afflicted mother.
Your sincere friend
A. Lincoln

Although his steadfast support for the abolition of slavery is clearly perched at the forefront of his character, what impresses me most about Lincoln was his humble attitude and determination. Even when he lost elections; when loved ones died young, including his mother, younger brother and older brother, his first love, Ann Rutledge, he would bounce back and hold on with anvil determination to fight for what was right. He was not on good terms with his father and did not even attend his funeral as Lincoln was apparently abused on some level we will never know. In the letter above, he writes condolences as a man that constantly fought depression. He took what he knew about fighting a battle (severe depression) and shared it with a young woman who lost her father.

King David came from a similar and unlikely background and rose to be the greatest leader of Israel. He was chosen as a shepherd with no formal education. Being the youngest in a large family, there would likely be little in the way of an inheritance. But the heart of David was what pleased God. Although he made mistakes that would change his household forever, he never stopped loving and serving God.

Our snapshot of David is that of an old man, ready to die, who needed to get his final arrangements in order. He had gone from underdog, to armor bearer, to general, to king and reigned for 40 years. The throne should have gone to Adonija, David's first legitimate son but we see, again, that God intervenes just as He did in making David king after Saul died.

Focus Scripture: 1 Kings 1:11-12

> "…Have you not heard that Adonijah the son of Haggith has become king, and David our lord does not know it? So now come, please let me give you counsel and save your life and the life of your son Solomon."

Focus Scripture: 1 Kings 1:50

> "And Adonijah was afraid of Solomon, and he arose, went and took hold of the horns of the altar."

Focus Scripture: 1 Kings 1:52

> "And Solomon said, 'if he will be a worthy man, not one of his hairs will fall to the ground; but if wickedness is found in him, he will die.'"

If Adonijah would have become king instead of Solomon, we can be fairly certain that Solomon would have been executed. Instead, Solomon offers loving kindness to his half brother. Solomon demonstrated great compassion on Adonijah as his little army of followers quickly vanished when they learned about Solomon being given the thrown. Instead of damnation, Adonijah received a second chance. Christ offers the same kind of love and reconciliation to us and takes us from the pits of despair and offers us another chance and another day.

The new-age people would like us to believe that we are "kings" in our own right, taking positive self-esteem to the point of self-worship. Solomon promised that if Adonijah was worthy, not one hair would fall. Adonijah could have repented but evil and jealousy gripped his heart and he was eventually executed (Chapter 2). It must have been a heart-breaking experience for Solomon to see his brother executed and so it is when Christ sees one of the lost die without ever coming to a relationship with Him.

What virtues did Solomon have that were learned from his father?

What sculptures wisdom?

How is punishment inflicted on us?

Day 22: Free in the big house

Scripture - Philippians 1:1-30

When I was 13 years old I used to pray at night that God would take my life. I was a confused young man who had accepted Christ but was not sure about the destiny of life on this planet. As I write these words, I look forward to this day. The rain will let up after a healthy thunder storm, the clouds will melt in the summer sun, I may call my son or daughter, and my wife and I will probably visit the local arboretum. What a contrast from the young man that lay in bed wondering why the cycle of life was allowed to torment him!

Paul saw all life, here and hereafter, to be a gift and challenge from God. If he were free from prison, he saw life as an opportunity to visit or plant churches. If he were imprisoned he saw it as a chance to share the gospel with the downcast of his day and write letters to the churches and people that were continuing a ministry. He was challenged by others who were also promoting Christ and his response was to let it happen if it expands the realm of believers. He looked at death as a final process of human life and the beginning of servitude in heaven.

Focus Scripture: Philippians 1: 9-11

"And this is my prayer: that your love may abound more and more in knowledge and depth of insight, so that you may be able to discern what is best and may be pure and blameless until the day of Christ, filled with the fruit of righteousness that comes through Jesus Christ – to the glory and praise of God."

Focus Scripture: Philippians 1:12

"Now, I want you to know, brethren that my circumstances have turned out for the greater progress of the gospel."

Focus Scripture: Philippians 1: 23, 24

"But I am hard-pressed from both directions, having the desire to depart and be with Christ, for that is very much better; yet to remain on in the flesh is more necessary for your sake."

Buried in the middle of the sports section of this morning's paper was a headline "Ex-reliever Howe dies at 48 in truck wreck." Steve Howe was named rookie of the year in 1980 as he had 17 saves for the Los Angeles Dodgers. But his career was derailed and blistered with alcohol and cocaine use. The paper went on to say that at age 39 he tried to make a comeback in the minor league but quit mid-season because of an injury. If one reads between the lines, Steve Howe was tormented and successful at the same time. He probably thought his purpose in life was to pitch baseballs and save games. Perhaps he was irritated with feelings of inadequacy because he was not a regular starting pitcher. I do not know but I know that he had a hard life, perhaps without a relationship with Christ. Instead of being hard-pressed in all directions to serve God, he was hard pressed from an inward direction to find a purpose in life.

We are not here on this planet without a purpose. I am an ambassador, away from my majestic home in heaven but I have work to do. I am the Lords and I cannot lose. My circumstances of both joy and despair are ever changing but nothing is by chance and everything is by divine will and the will of God is that I share Christ in some capacity on a daily basis. I am the best person here in this place and time to perform that job. If it were not so, God would have sent someone else. As the rains taper off and the morning thunder dissipates, I can only marvel at a God who has a plan in every molecule of matter made. The universe was created by intelligent design with heart-felt care for all of us. Every breath we take has purpose.

We merely have to recognize the substance of our existence that is sourced from a God who truly loves us.

Thinking back on some of the characters of the Bible, what circumstances might they have been in that would cause them to despair?

Cocaine and alcohol abuse are just one way of mishandling life. What other attitudes or circumstances can interfere with us seeing our purpose?

If you look at the first chapter of Philippians, how did Paul deal with his adversaries?

The purpose of today is to _____
_____.

State any other observations you made about Paul's letter to the Philippians.

Day 23: Who do you call?

Scripture – II Kings 1:1-18

I am embarrassed about many things I have done during my life but one glaring incident occurred at a coffee shop during my sophomore year in college. A group of us decided that it would be kind of fun to channel the devil so we sat in a circle on the floor and locked at the elbows and one of the members of the group started inviting Satan to join us. It was a huge mistake. After a short time the fire went out in the fireplace and a very cold wind moved out of the hearth into the room. We all were terrified and immediately turned on all the lights and swore never to do it again. The reader can judge this to be a back draft from the flue but I must exclaim that the cold draft that chilled us seemed to come from all sides. What was I thinking? But, in those times, I was not very well grounded in scripture and was a pretty immature Christian in so many ways.

The entire incident seems harmless but many people have gone from encounters of this sort, to cults that lay ownership of their entire existence. One such cult was started by a man named David Koresh. His name will fade with history but the occurrence at Waco, Texas will drone on for years. On April 19, 1993, FBI agents attempted to end a stand-off and in the process the Davidian compound caught fire and 80 people perished in a mysterious disaster. His followers believed he was a Christ and they sought enlightenment through his teachings and rituals. They are people that were searching for truth and happiness through the wrong source.

Focus Scripture: II Kings 1:2

"And Ahaziah fell through the lattice in his upper chamber which was in Samaria, and became ill. So he sent messengers and said to them, 'Go, inquire of Baal-zebub the god of Ekron, whether I shall recover from this sickness.'"

Focus Scripture: II Kings 1:6

"'A man came to meet us," they replied, "And he said to us, "Go back to the king who sent you and tell him, "This is what the Lord says: Is it because there is no God in Israel that you are sending men to consult Baal-Zebub, the god of Ekron?" Therefore you will not leave the bed you are lying on. You will certainly die!"'"

Focus Scripture: II Kings 1:14

"Behold fire came down from heaven, and consumed the first two captains of fifty with their fifties but now let my life be precious in your sight."

When King Ahaziah was sick, he sought a prognosis related to his recovery. Instead of seeking healing through prayer, he sought a foreign god to prophesy. He was flirting with both physical and spiritual death and dealt with it by employing foreign gods instead of the One living God who delivered the country of his leadership. Along with his own spiritual illness came the death of two brigades that were consumed with fire because they were seeking to apprehend Elijah. Finally, the leader of a third brigade recognized the hand of God and pleaded for the life of his troops. Whether the fear of God or fear for their lives lead them to this state of confession makes little difference. If Ahaziah had asked God for forgiveness and healing, he would have been made well, spiritually. Instead, he was subject to eternal torment and took people with him.

The reality of this story is that people want leadership and they desire something or someone to believe in. They often turn to tarot cards and mysticism instead of Christ and the example of His life of leadership. The state of being totally removed from God is one of choice and not circumstances. We make decisions to drift away in small increments. We allow ourselves to read trash, watch bad things on television, align ourselves with non-believing friends and finally entertain a belief system that is totally contrary to the God-fearing one that saved us. In that process, we hurt ourselves and others along the way. Children rebel, marriages drift apart, drugs and alcohol dismantle us physically. All this happens because we exchange the truth for deception.

The night I was at the coffee shop at college and allowed myself to experiment with Satan was a turning point in life. To tell the truth, God allowed our group to drift away into the coldness of Satan and the death of the fire in the fireplace seemed to represent isolation in hell. That night I returned home and committed to read my Bible and walk in His daily grace instead of living a double standard. Not long afterwards, I met the love of my life and I was prepared to assume a leadership role as husband, and eventually, Daddy.

How does the fear of God's wrath and the Love of Christ work together to draw us closer to a relationship with Him?

How does the folly of this life lead people away from the One living God?

How can we avoid deception?

Day 24: From the floor up

Scripture – Colossians 1: 1-29; 2:2-3

We bought a house in Texas in 2005. Before closing on the house, an inspection had to be performed. The thorough inspection involved checking everything from the outside weep holes, to the shingles, to the hot water heater. Finally, the inspector ran a bubble level on the first floor. The apparatus was positioned in about the center of the house and a hose filled with liquid was moved to various corners of the house to check the slab for irregular elevations. The slab for our home was so level that no aberrations were detected, meaning that every point on the slab was within 0.1 inches! The house has problems with the wall texturing and some pealing paint but the frame is on a perfectly level slab. That means that I can be reasonably sure that all the walls are at 90 degrees from the perfectly level slab. I can show these results to the next buyer and he or she can check out the slab for themselves.

This is the kind of faith that we have. It is squarely built on nothing less than a perfect plan that goes from one room called "creation of the world," to another room called "forgiveness," to another room called "sovereignty of God," to another room called the "Future." All the rooms fit together on a firm and level slab. There may be irregularities that we put there as we build our lives on trials and errors, represented by pealing paint, but the house still stands.

The snapshots that Paul left us were in the form of letters that dealt with these irregularities caused by differences in culture, points of contention between gentile and Jew, varying economic brackets, and prevailing philosophies of the time. So when Paul wrote to the Colossians, he was reminding them that there was nothing wrong with the slab on which their beliefs had been founded but he also had to set the congregation straight on why he was an authority, representing the builder. The letter to the Colossians put the level down in each room and established the security of God's ultimate building plan.

Focus Scripture: Colossians 1:9

> "For this reason also, since the day we heard of it, we have not ceased to pray for you and to ask that you may be filled with the knowledge of His will in all spiritual wisdom and understanding."

Focus Scripture: Colossians 1:17

> "And He is before all things and in Him all things hold together."

Focus Scripture: Colossians 1:22

> "Yet He has now reconciled you in His fleshy body through death, in order to present you before Him holy and blameless and beyond reproach."

Focus Scripture: 2:2

> " that their hearts may be encouraged, having been knit together in love, and attaining to all the wealth that comes from the full assurance of understanding, resulting in a true knowledge of God's mystery, that is, Christ himself."

One day we will present the building of our lives before God and Christ will testify for us and say this building is beyond reproach. We may say to ourselves "yeah, but there were some things I did that were very reproachable." But the plan of salvation presents us as a blameless creation. Just as the very elements hold together at God's command, so does the building plan for our lives, in spite of our transgressions. Through the Holy Spirit, I realize that Christ himself was with God in the beginning, engaging a plan of salvation. I am cleansed daily by God so that I will be able to bow before the throne of the Great Carpenter.

It is hard to believe that we could mess up a design so perfect and level. Looking back on the previous account (Day 23), I wonder how I could ever take the shoddy construction of my own life and become an heir to Jesus. But it is His all encompassing grace that plumbs the walls. Unlike a building that we put together that can shift and falter, the house that God builds for us is on level and firm footing.

Some of the Christians of the early church believed that of salvation was mysteriously revealed through personal enlightenment, to the point that they sometimes separated themselves from other believers who thought otherwise. This was the basis of Gnostic writings that circulated in the first couple of centuries after Christ ascended. As you look at the word "mystery" in verse 27 (Chapter 1) and verse 2 (Chapter 2), what message is Paul trying to convey to Gnostic believers?

Read verse 21 again and contemplate what is meant by the terminology "hostile in mind, engaged in evil deeds."

How can we bolster Paul's efforts mentioned in verse 25?

Take your own snapshots (make observations) regarding this insightful scripture.

Day 25: To lose a kingship

Scripture: 1 Chronicles 10: 1-14

We have to marvel at the plan of salvation. Almost everyone has heard of the thieves on the cross next to Jesus. One cried out to our Lord and the other did not. At some point in our lives we will no longer be able to cry out from our conscience and for those who do not have a relationship with God, it will be too late. Before that time God is patient with us. God was extremely patient with Saul but there came a point when the king could not bring himself to trust in God.

Saul started out as a good king with the blessings of God. He was initially obedient to the commandments. But the man, Saul, started to feed on the king, Saul. And when anyone seeks after themselves for all wisdom, pleasure, and self righteousness, then they will find themselves in disfavor with God. Once we stray from the true righteousness of God, we start to make our religion conform to our own distorted conscience. We could even make Jesus a small part of the belief but facet the religion around our own rules that we make up as life goes on. That is what happened to Saul and God hated it and the lineage of kingship was turned over to an obscure family in Bethlehem. From that unlikely house of Jesse sprang a root of faith that culminated with the miraculous birth, ministry, and resurrection of King Jesus.

Focus Scripture: 1 Chronicles 10: 6, 7

> "...Saul and his three sons died, and all his house died together. When all the Israelites in the valley saw that the army had fled and that Saul and his sons had died, they abandoned their towns and fled. And the Philistines came and occupied them."

Focus Scripture: 1 Chronicles 10: 13-14

> "So Saul died for his trespass which he committed against the Lord, because of the word of the Lord which he did not keep; and also, because he asked counsel of a medium, making inquiry of it, and did not inquire of the Lord. Therefore, He killed him, and turned the kingdom to David the son of Jesse."

When Saul took his own life, and the heirs to the throne were also killed, there appeared to be a victory for the Philistines and the end of the great Hebrew nation. But God had a promise and a plan for David to be spliced into the leadership of Judah. As we take a final snap shot of Saul and David, we can reflect on the fact that there is a point when one can no longer repent and turn around. An automobile may take a life or a person could intentionally overdose and then there is no time to turn our heads to Jesus and ask, "remember me in paradise."

We think of Saul as a wicked King. He broke every commandment and turned to a customized religion, trying to fit his own deception into a self-serving sphere. But, he started out as the anointed King. His fall hurts as we see what course free-will can take.

Was the destruction of Saul the plan of God so that David could be installed as King?

Pray for someone who is on a collision course and make a commitment to be involved in their lives.

Day 26: Get a tune-up

Scripture - 1 Thessalonians 1:1 – 2:3

Before the days of electronic ignition and fuel injection, in order for a car to run well, it needed a properly adjusted carburetor and spark delivered to the cylinders at the precise moment as dictated by the magneto and the distributor. Many of us non-mechanics would try to fix our own vehicles, especially when we were living on macaroni and cheese. Case in point, our 1976 Ford Pinto was not running well in spite of all efforts to change the plugs, sparkplug wires, and air filter. Finally, a mechanic told me that the car needed a new carburetor. At the time we could not afford one so I decided to fix it myself and, living in an apartment, the work was completed on the kitchen table. I was amazed at the simplicity and yet the marvelous design of the carburetor. It was rather fun to take it apart and follow the directions in the carburetor kit that eventually lead to the rebuilding of my own carburetor. When I installed it on the car and started the engine, the car still was not running quite right but, after a little adjustment and more running, the car ran like a top. The lesson is that it takes more than just spark and fuel to run a car it takes timing and the right gas/air mixture. A modern automobile requires the same timing and mixture, although it is done differently due to electronics and precise injection of fuel.

We can read our Bibles, go to church and Sunday School, but we are not running on all cylinders if we fail to rely on the Holy Spirit to guide our lives. Paul's letter to the Thessalonians bears instructions in this regard.

Focus Scripture: I Thessalonians 1: 4-5

> "For we know, brothers loved by God, that He has chosen you, because our gospel came to you not simply with words, but also with power, with the Holy Spirit and with deep conviction."

Focus Scripture: 1 Thessalonians 1: 8

> "And now the word of the Lord is ringing out from you to people everywhere, even beyond Greece, for wherever we go we find people telling us about your faith in God."

Focus Scripture: I Thessalonians 2: 2b

> "...but with the help of our God we dared to tell you His gospel in spite of strong opposition."

In our travels through life, we must call on the Holy Spirit to mix the spiritual gifts, spiritual discernment, and head knowledge of the Bible together in order that the Body of Christ runs well. In Paul's letter to the church of Thessalonica, he starts by praising the work started in them and explains why the new church has grown and why it will continue to do so. A Holy life is the best testimony of the great salvation that we have come to know but the future generation will confront the same opposition to the gospel and the same solution will be required in order for this vehicle of life to endure rejection. Just as the internal combustion engine has not changed since it was invented, so the same ingredients and combinations are necessary in order for us to feel the full impact of successful and secure Christian living. I have learned in my own walk with the Lord that when one piece of the mechanism fails it tends to fowl up the rest of the machinery. Prayer, Bible study, worship, fellowship and the carburetor of the Holy Spirit are all required parts of the Christian walk. We must blend the gospel with good works and breathe in the oxygen of the Holy Spirit in order to deliver the right message to the world around us.

What is your initial impression of the people of the Thessalonica?

How are we connected to our church, ideally and in reality?

Why is it important to us that the church be dynamic and changing; why is it important to our community?

If you were to build and automobile (symbolic of successful Christian living), what spiritual components would you make sure were incorporated into the car?

Pistons:
Carburetor:
Fuel:
Others:

Day 27: Electromagnetometers work

Scripture - II Chronicles: 1:1 to 2:1

Several years ago I was asked to use an electromagnetometer in order to survey a buried dump. This would not be a problem for an experienced geophysicist who understood the equipment and the process of collecting data. It was necessary to carry a 20 foot long tool through the brush and periodically record the magnetic field. Before the days of GPS, a compass and survey was necessary in order to correctly position the data. I thought this would be an impressive accomplishment and something worthy of documentation on my resume. But after several days with the rented tool, I finally realized that I did not have a clue what I was doing and the rental time of the equipment would soon lapse. I prayed for help but continued to fail and would sometimes waste an entire day in the woods with the hungry black flies feasting on my ears as I carried the heavy instrument through the brush, swamp and thick grassy fields.

What was wrong with my prayer? Solomon prayed for wisdom and was granted his request. I prayed and contracted poison ivy.

Focus Scripture: II Chronicles 1: 5-7

"Now the bronze altar, which Bezalel, the son of Uri, the son of Hur had made, was there before the tabernacle of the Lord, and Solomon and the assembly sought it out ...In that night God appeared to Solomon and said to him, 'ask what I shall give you.'"

Earl Fashbaugh

Focus Scripture: II Chronicles 1: 11-12

> "And God said to Solomon, because you had this in mind, and did not ask for riches, wealth, or honor, or the life of those who hate you, nor have you even asked for long life, but you have asked for yourself wisdom and knowledge, that you may rule My people, over who I have made you king, wisdom and knowledge have been granted to you, and I will give you riches and wealth and honor, such as none of the kings who were before you has possessed, nor those who will come after you."

Solomon first approached God with a worshipful heart as he sacrificed the best of his possessions to the Lord. Then he prayed and asked with very pure motives. His prayer was not lip service but was a sincere request that moved God to the point that He answered, "ask what I shall give you." God knew what Solomon was going to ask for and was ready to provide but wanted to hear the prayer that would trigger a great blessing.

Solomon was not asking for a blessing for himself. Rather, he carried a great burden to lead the country in a Godly manner. Solomon recognized that he was not by himself and that the greatest counselor was available to provide military, economic, and spiritual guidance. We see a model for prayer and leadership that can be applied to our immediate families and all the way to the White House. Solomon was living the Lord's prayer before Jesus appeared on the earth where he prayerfully approached God and said in his own words, "Our Father who is in Heaven, Holy is your Name."

As for the geologist who could not get the magnetometer to work, he had to search his heart for the reason of his failure in order to find a means of success. I had to humble myself before my supervisor whom I did not get along with, and start calling on the manufacturing company to learn how to use the instrument. Once this was accomplished and a prayer was submitted to God asking for wisdom in running the instrument, then the task fell easily in place. The survey was done ahead of schedule and the rented equipment sent back on time. I had to surrender a zeal for myself and render a desire to serve my employer for the cause of identifying environmental hazards buried beneath the surface of the ground.

Similarly, when we ask God to reveal the treasure and the trash of our lives, He is quick to do so because that is the ultimate prayer that He is waiting for. If our motives are to serve others, God rarely turns anyone down. He may say, "later" but he embraces us and our requests when we put Godly motives first. The complex instrumentation of our lives is like a cumbersome magnetometer that needs calibration through prayer in order to become an asset to those around us; in order to make the days we live have a full impact on others.

When Jesus said, "My yoke is easy and my burden is light" (Matthew 11:30) He was emphasizing that a life in Christ bears a yoke. We do not get by without responsibility and the need to be credible. But the burden is light compared to living with the entire load of items that we may try to tote around without a clue of what we are, where we are going, or what divine purpose we have.

Why do evil people sometimes amass tremendous wealth when their motives are selfish?

Why do Godly people amass blessings that put God first in their lives?

As we think about something that we would like to have, what is the reason for this and what alternative could we ask for that would be more aligned with the will of God?

Why was Solomon chosen to build the temple instead of his father, David?

Record any other personality traits that Solomon had that were augmented by his prayer?

Day 28: A good gardener

Scripture - II Thessalonians 1: 1-12; 2: 1-4

Gardening is not one of my virtues. When spring comes, I can usually find the enthusiasm to buy the seed and will turn the sleeping soil. There is great satisfaction in preparing the ground to receive the seed by raking the surface and planning the rows. But, something usually goes wrong when my ten green thumbs attempt to plant the little miracle seeds. I plant them too deep or too shallow or too close together. At first, I weed the garden on a daily basis but after about 3 weeks, I lose interest and in due time it becomes difficult to see where the "fruits" of my labor were once dedicated. Weeds choke out the crop and another harvest is avoided.

Paul, on the other hand, was a great gardener. He kept the rows well tended and weeded the garden in a timely manor. He had several gardens to tend, one of them being the church in Thessalonica. His second letter to the Thessalonians was apparently written because some false teachings and misunderstandings were springing up among the healthy plants that were growing spiritually. Although God ultimately causes the garden to grow, He also wants us to tend the garden and be involved in the weeding process.

Focus Scripture: II Thessalonians 1: 3

> "We ought always to give thanks to God for you, brethren, as is only fitting, because your faith is greatly enlarged, and the love of each one of you toward one another grows ever greater..."

Earl Fashbaugh

Focus Scripture: II Thessalonians 1: 11-12

"With this in mind, we constantly pray for you, that our God may count you worthy of His calling, and that by His power He may fulfill every good purpose of yours and every act prompted by your faith. We pray this that the name of Jesus may be glorified in you..."

Focus Scripture: II Thessalonians 2: 1-3

"Concerning the coming of our Lord Jesus Christ and our being gathered to him, we ask you, brothers, not to become easily unsettled or alarmed by some prophecy, report or letter supposed to have come from us, saying that the day of the Lord has already come. Don't let anyone deceive you in any way..."

Our gardener, Paul, was quick to take care of the good plants and provide encouragement. He told them they were doing well and supported their growth and further reminded them that through faith and prayers a binding element of love would ultimately lead to a great harvest. But he also reminded them that the harvest time was dictated by God and that the plants do not control the garden. The plants find their purpose by sending roots down into the rich nutrients of scripture, fellowship, and continuous prayer. Similar to the snapshot of Solomon (Day 27), we see that every good purpose demands attention to the garden and not passive interest in the harvest time. Life requires watering with love in order to encourage true spiritual wisdom, directed at fellow-plants, whether they are the entire church or the people that attend.

My literal garden looks pretty sick. The lettuce never did come up, the squash is dwarfed, and only a few carrots may mature. Meanwhile, there is a hedge of grass perched on the outside of the garden, casting a shadow on the plants that are struggling to attain son-light. Some of the weeds have sent little runners into the garden so that it is hard to distinguish the fruitful plants from the intruders. A good gardener knows what is needed to keep the plants growing and maturing. So it is with any church program. Growth will "supersede" evil if the love of Christ is administered continuously. As for the weeds, God has asked us to take part in the cleansing and tending of this garden but come the harvest, we will let Him deal with the ungodly.

The gospel stands on its own, without additional doctrine. Paul warns us all that deception is creeping near our gardens, trying to choke out the truth or at least confuse us from knowing the difference between good fruit and destructive ideas. Through prayer, fellowship, and Biblical examination, we should identify the "man of lawlessness" (II Thes. 2:3) who would like nothing more than to mess up our garden.

As we take snapshots of Solomon's prayer for wisdom in leading the nation, how may this picture compare to the local church? What level of leadership should we function at?

Are we the plants or the gardener?

Reading between the lines in Thessalonians, what may have been some problems in the church that would have precipitated Paul's second letter?

Day 29: Temple treasures

Scripture – Ezra: Chapter 1: 1-11

We leaped from David to Solomon and are now taking a snapshot of a fallen nation. Once a power to be reckoned with, Israel was a shamble and the people were deported. The Hebrews went from slavery in Egypt to freedom and a beautiful place of worship in Jerusalem, back to slavery in Babylonia. One generation did not remember the one before and the nation Israel went full circle back to captivity.

Our family as lived in 21 different homes in 35 years of marriage. We seem to scarcely have time to cut the grass before it is time to pick up our suitcase and move again but we now have a retirement home in focus. It represents the return to a place close to where we fell in love and a journey to a real home. This is the emotion that filled the heart of a single man, Ezra, for restoration of a homeland and spiritual restoration of a nation. The same kind of return to a "home" that we love happens when we realize that we have been living outside of the real will of God. We wonder why we find ourselves so far away from our home and first love, and then rejoice at our coming back to the roots of our spiritual heritage.

Focus Scripture: Ezra 1: 4

"And every survivor, at whatever place he may live, let the men of that place support him with silver and gold, with goods and cattle together with a freewill offering for the house of God which is in Jerusalem."

Focus Scripture Ezra 1:7

> "King Cyrus himself brought out the valuable items which King Nebuchadnezzar had taken from the Lord's temple in Jerusalem and had placed in the temple of his own gods."

After 70 years of slavery, many of the Hebrews did not even know what a nation they once had. God changed their attitudes and even changed the attitude of the oppressive government that held them hostage. King Cyrus was changed to the point that he gave back the plunder of a former regime. The items that were in the Temple would return with the people and full restoration was decreed.

Everyone has their own Jerusalem. It is that special place that God wants us to be. If we try to grab the reins away from God or we refuse to move when God wants us to go somewhere else, we lose our effectiveness as Christians. Indeed, we lose our identity and plunge ourselves into slavery of this world. But, through all our inadequacy, God is able to transform us and the situation but it requires a prayer and rendering of the reins back to Jesus, our first love.

We have a part in the cleansing process. Just as King Cyrus had to remove the plunder from the temple, we must throw out the some items that may have ruled a former life. Some of the trophies that were important to us at one time can interfere with the offerings that we bring today. Temple purification keeps our thoughts aligned with the will of God.

What is Supernatural about returning to our Lord when we have been off in our own selfish ambitions?

What kind of obstacles did the Nation Israel have to overcome in order to return to Jerusalem and how could these barriers be compared to us returning to a life style that is consistent with our faith?

Day 30: Actors need not apply

Scripture – I Timothy 1: 1-20

There is one outstanding highlight that clearly is perched as the hallmark of my senior year in high school and that moment came when I was cast as the King in "The King and I." Several students participated, including the entire school orchestra. I was surrounded by some very nice looking girls and was playing a role of authority. The performance ran three nights and I recall the evening after the first show how I cruised up and down the streets of Forest Lake in my old rusty car, radio blaring, with the muffler dragging and making a horrendous noise. But, it was a moment that I will not forget. I was brought quickly down to reality as I looked in the rear view mirror and heard a siren from the local police. With make-up still on, I rolled down the window and copied a line from my father, "what seems to be the problem, officer?" He glared at me and asked, "who do you think you are?" All I could offer was, "I am the King of Siam." We had a lengthy conversation after that; so much for being an authority. I was told to get my 'royal "hindest" home.'

Paul's letter to Timothy addresses the "actors" of our faith. In our walk with Christ, there can be no acting or make up. We must control our every conversation so that we are consistent with the character of Christ.

Focus Scripture: I Timothy 1:5,6

> "But the goal of our instruction is to love from a pure heart and a good conscience and a sincere faith. For some men straying from these things, have turned aside to fruitless discussion."

Focus Scripture: I Timothy 1:17

> "Now to the King eternal, immortal, invisible, the only God, be honor and glory forever and ever. Amen."

Focus Scripture: I Timothy 1:19

> "Cling tightly to your faith in Christ, and always keep your conscience clear. For some people have deliberately violated their consciences; as a result, their faith has been shipwrecked."

There is an old saying in the business world, "it's not what you know but who you know." As Christians this is true in that we know Jesus but we must also know someone else. We must know ourselves. If the instruction or the code of ethics comes from anything but a pure, loving and sincere faith in Christ, it is a doctrine of destruction. Only the "King eternal" deserves our focused attention and only those who promote Him are worthy to be our instructors. Anyone who proposes to have authority, and does not wear the badge of love, looks about as foolish as I did the night after the first performance. Praise God for understanding cops who send us in the right direction – home.

Why do we feel shipwrecked when we depart from our consciences as Christians?

Do we ever put on "make up" of unbelievers?

Day 31: Help wanted, Administrator

Scripture – Nehemiah 1:1-11

This first chapter in Nehemiah is so packed with practical lessons on living a Godly life that it would be impossible to summarize the implications in one or two paragraphs. The flow of the scripture is as follows:

First, we learn about decay in our lives;
- We ask for forgiveness;
- We pray for others in spite of our situation;
- We ask for knowledge;
- Listen to what God has us do, and
- Act according to the will of God.

You cannot frame a house before the foundation is poured anymore than you can assume a roll as leader before you have been a great follower of instruction.

Focus Scripture: Nehemiah 1: 4-6

"As soon as I heard these words I sat down and wept and mourned for days, and I continued fasting and praying before the God of heaven. And I said 'O Lord God of heaven, the great and awesome God who keeps covenant and steadfast love with those who love him and keep his commandments, let your ear be attentive and your eyes open, to hear the prayer of your servant that I now pray before you day and night for the people of Israel your servants, confessing the sins of the people of Israel, which we have sinned against you. Even I and my father's house have sinned.'"

Focus Scripture: Nehemiah 1:11

"Oh Lord, let your ear be attentive to the prayer of this your servant and the prayer of your servants who delight in revering your name. Give your servant success today by granting him favor in the presence of this man."

Anyone who may happen to read the "focus scripture" without reading the entire chapter, and, perhaps the entire book of Nehemiah, may miss the point of this prayer. Nehemiah, the trusted servant and cupbearer of the earthly king was asking the eternal King that he would be successful in helping the people of God come together to once again worship Him and know the protection of His grace. The motives are strikingly similar to those of King Solomon seeking wisdom in leading his nation. This time the prayer comes from a hard working but respected servant who cares more about the return to morality and a relationship with the Lord than he cares about himself.

A combination of people worked together to repair the wall around Jerusalem. Day 29 was devoted another individual, Ezra. While Nehemiah provided the administrative leadership, Ezra was a spiritual leader for which the footing of the wall was positioned. All good leaders start out as good servants and we learn to apply our abilities by looking far outside of our own sphere of abilities.

The snapshot of people building a wall contains people of diverse talents. How is this similar to our efforts to build a secure church?

If you saw yourself in a snapshot of workers who helped build a spiritual wall of protection, what would you say your talent is and how you contribute to the process of building?

Day 32: Wagon Wheels

Scripture – II Timothy 1: 1-18

It is called the Oregon Trail. Wagon trains, heading west, with people trying to find a new life, left an impression on this country in both a literal and figurative sense. One can still see the ruts left by the thousands of wagon wheels that crossed Wyoming. A tingling feeling falls over me to look at this historical trace that is etched in the soil, still there even though over a hundred years have passed. I can't help but to think about the insecurity that these people must have felt, thinking about the homes they left and not knowing what lies over the mountain or across the sage brush plains. These people probably left an impression on their children too, an impression of perseverance and endurance; many of those offspring are alive today, living in the western and coastal states. They never knew their great-great-great grandparents but they do know the lesson, the example. Paul writes about this generation-to-generation example in his final letter to Timothy.

Focus Scripture: II Timothy 1:5,6

> "For I am mindful of the sincere faith within you, which first dwelt in your grandmother, Lois, and your mother Eunice, and I am sure that it is in you as well. And for this reason I remind you to kindle afresh the gift of God that is in you through the laying on of hands."

Focus Scripture: II Timothy 1:13

> "Retain the standard of sound words which you have heard from me, in the faith and love which are in Christ Jesus."

Did Timothy actually know his own grandmother? Paul apparently knew her by name, Lois. In Biblical times it was probably rare that a person would remember their grandparents and often times this generation would have died long before the grandchildren were conceived. The faith that Timothy had was, in part, attributed to his grandmother and mother. From one generation to the next Paul reminds us to carry the standard of sound words, the wagon wheels of faith and love in Christ. I am thankful for all the people who have come and gone from my life. I have taken bits and pieces of each of them and my own personality and Christian instruction is built from those people.

Every day the wagon wheels turn and the soil of people around us is impacted by where we have been in their lives. We cannot see the impression anymore than someone would as they journeyed in their covered wagon. But, day by day, moment by moment we take turns leaving a lasting legacy of love etched on a trail leading to eternal life.

Who has had the biggest, positive influence on your life and how is that manifest in yours?

Do you get the impression that Paul feels that these may be his last words of instruction to the young man, Timothy?

Day 33: The queen of hearts

Scripture – Esther 1:1 to 2:3

Referring back to Day 32, I think of my long-departed mother, whose name was Esther. She was a Godly woman that insisted on me attending Sunday School even though I had other aspirations, especially in the summer. She was next, a devoted wife to my father for 49 years. Next, she was a mother with energy, always wanting to make sure that we were loved and well cared for. Finally, she was a nurse who took her work seriously as a service to God. There were times when her work as an RN came first and the order of priorities shifted from day to day but she always put herself last. She never made demands on my Dad, although my father was quick to honor her requests, especially during the last years of her life.

It remains a mystery to me how she would fix my favorite meals when I came home from college and still maintain her administrative position at the hospital. She was a servant of our Lord and in so many ways she pays tribute to the namesake of this unusual Bible Book we call "Esther." We may take a snapshot of this Book but it really must be read in one sitting to fully realize the significance of a story about a Godly woman. Paradoxically, the Book of Esther never really mentions God but does dwell on doing the right thing and being an obedient servant. Through this obedience, consequences of our actions fit together in an understanding manner.

The book of Esther is about a beautiful woman who becomes queen. She hides her identity as a Jew from the Persian King but is willing to give her life and reveal this heritage. In doing this she averted a holocaust of

Jews everywhere from present day Iraq to Egypt. Esther was raised by her uncle so she was likely an orphan, raised from humble beginnings to royalty. Through this, she remained faithful to God and put Him first, even knowing that she could be executed. There are many parallels here. For example, our Lord followed through and set up His own execution so that we could be saved from condemnation.

Focus Scripture – Esther 2:15

> "Now when the turn came for Esther, the daughter of Abihail the uncle of Mordecai who had taken her as his daughter, came to go in to the king, she did not request anything except what Hegai, the king's eunuch who was in charge of the women, advised. And Esther found favor in the eyes of all who saw her."

If asked, to explain her faith, Esther would have been honest about her Jewish background. She wanted to protect her family as the Jews were hated by the controlling Persian kingdom. Sadly, the same kind of hatred prevails in that region of the world today and Jews and Christians, alike, are persecuted for their beliefs.

Mom died of cancer in 1987. She would tell my Dad that the worst part about being sick is that she could not do things for him and other people. She was a Godly woman in many ways. Oh, she didn't preach the gospel all the time but there was no question about her conviction and her resolve to put the feelings of others before her own. This Book of Esther is about doing what you can to help the oppressed (in this case, the Jewish nation). In my mother's case, it meant spreading goodwill to everyone around her. I sure miss Mom but she would tell me to do something for someone else and quit thinking about her.

What kind of characteristics would a woman like Esther have?

Esther allowed herself to become queen without telling the king that she was Jewish. How can this be a part of God's plan when deceit is involved?

What is our message as Christians in a pagan world?

What other snapshots would you take of this unusual book?

Day 34: Tribute to a special elder

Scripture – Titus 1:1 to 2:10

My Father-in-law is an elder in the Biblical sense. He is too old to serve an active administration position but there can be no doubt about the leadership role that God has given him. He is smart but not brilliant; he knows how to make a point but he is not a great statesman. He can get angry but he always exercises control and would never hurt anyone physically or emotionally, although he can give a ribcrushing hug to just about anyone. He is overfilled with love and reads the Word of God daily. In every sense of the word, he is an elder because he has a pure heart and genuine love for the Lord. I have been asked to serve as an elder for two different churches and I have reflected on the man who gave me a wife that will always be at my side to show her support and continue to the heritage of love

Focus Scripture Titus1:6, 7

> "…if anyone is above reproach, the husband of one wife, and his children are believers and not open to the charge of debauchery or insubordination. For an overseer, as God's Stewart, must be above reproach. He must not be arrogant or quick-tempered or a drunkard or violent or greedy for gain…"

Focus Scripture: Titus 1:9

> "...holding fast the faithful word which is in accordance with the teaching, that he may be able both to exhort in sound doctrine and to refute those who contradict."

Focus Scripture: Titus 2:5

> "...to be sensible, pure, workers at home, kind, being subject to their own husbands, that the word of God may not be dishonored."

The third focus scripture has to do with the conduct of a wife but it is every bit as applicable to the man. Our goal must always be purity, even in adversity. One does not consciously decide to become an elder. One becomes an elder by devoting time and energy promoting the gospel and by tending the sheep of His flock. Whether man or woman, young or old, the key to leadership is having a firm grasp of the Word and allowing the Holy Spirit have total control. Paul appointed some people as elders of the church and today we sometimes appoint elders in our congregations but a true, Biblical elder is recognized by all, without appointment or voting. My father-in-law had four children; all of them Christian and all married to Christian spouses. He is an elder, because through his example, he has passed the baton to another generation.

As I edit these words, my father-in-law, Gene Monroe, has severe dementia such that he no longer cares much about his hair or clothes. He is pretty quiet but if you look into his eyes you will see a man that has great peace with God. These are the leaders that are sought in today's church. Some are administrative geniuses but many are spiritual warriors who pray for those around them. Similar to day 33, they are like Esther, putting others first. Jesus is the ultimate example.

How can we become better leaders in our church?

What should our response be if we are called to be leaders?

How is leadership of a corporation different than leadership of a church?

Day 35: Job applications

Scripture – Job 1:1 to 2:13

The book of Job is packed with applications about facing adversity, dealing with personal crisis, and recognizing the sovereignty of God. There are examples of wisdom and foolishness, often in the same chapter. We all know characters like Job and most of us will endure some point in our lives when we identify with him. A contemporary story of Job may go something like this:

Dick Sterling was a successful lawyer who owned a law firm in Minneapolis. He was well liked by many and had an impeccable reputation for honesty and fairness. He turned down many cases, mostly because of ethical reasons. Dick was a Christian and strong leader in his church. He served on committees to minister to the homeless and disadvantaged individuals and was assistant coach for the Little League baseball team. He was the model of success.

He and his wife Sharon had large family consisting of ten children, seven boys, and three girls in nearly thirty years of marriage. Two of the sons worked with their father at the law firm. The family was extremely wealthy, not just from the law firm, but from a long history of success dating back to the early days of iron mining in Minnesota.

God was busy tending the Universe when Satan appeared to be coming out of a black hole.

"What are you up to?" God inquired.

Satan retrieved a comb from his silk pants and started to tend his hair and replied, "Hey, Man, I've been doing my thing on earth."

"That's the only truth to come out of you," God said. "Have you seen my child Dick Sterling? There's a guy you'll never penetrate."

Satan let out a shrieking laugh and replied, "Well, I could make him curse you and this whole stinking universe. All I would have to do is take some of the soft living he has enjoyed away and you would see a pretty sick looking soul. I could even get him to blaspheme the Holy Spirit and..."

"That's enough," God said, with a blunt gesture as if he were stopping traffic. "Try as you want but you do not have custody of his physical life." Satan scurried off immediately and summoned his demons.

Dick and his wife were preparing to leave for the Lake Side Country Club from their Edina home when the phone rang. They were already running late when Dick picked up the phone.

"Hello. Yes, this is Dick Sterling."

Dick was informed by a policeman that a tornado touched down in the vicinity of the Country Club and that a gas line was ignited causing a horrendous explosion. At least 100 hundred people are dead, all of his children he would learn later.

Dick was in a state of shock when the IRS called moments later. He was informed that some "irregularities" were found on his past five income tax returns. All bank accounts were instantly frozen and his house was to be auctioned off next month. The audit would occur next week regardless of personal circumstances. Word of Dick's situation hit the credit bureau and all creditors demanded full payment.

Suddenly, for the first time in his life Dick was without money. All his children lay in state at Johnson Funeral Home but nothing was done to their bodies, pending an investigation.

Dick lowered his head in prayer and said, "Lord, you alone understand this circumstance. I alone, can never comprehend it. But, I know that you are Lord. Why have you done this?"

With tears streaming down his face he reached for his wife who just stared into space, in complete physical and emotional shock.

"Why don't you just die?" she said in rage and tears.

Focus Scripture: Job 1:20-21

"Then Job stood up, tore his robe and shaved his head. He fell to the ground and worshiped, 'Naked I came from my mother's womb, and naked I will leave this life. The Lord gives, and the Lord takes away. Praise the name of the Lord.'"

Focus Scripture: Job 1:22

"Through all this Job did not sin nor did he blame God."

Focus Scripture: Job 2:10b

"'Shall we indeed accept good from God and not accept adversity?' In all this, Job did not sin with his lips."

My wife and I know someone who lost both sons in a foolish automobile accident. The driver of the other vehicle had been drinking and smoking marijuana before the deadly headon collision occurred. If God was in control, why did He let something like this happen? I will never forget the look on the face of the father in the hospital who had just lost his two sons in an accident with his wife in critical condition (she lived). Later he moved to Atlanta where he started a new business and became even more successful. This did not bring his boys back but then, we cannot ever know what could have become of his sons.

Job was not a fictional character; nor was the story about the automobile accident. The father and husband who lost his wife and children was a type of Job, tested beyond our comprehension as he sat there in the hospital wondering what God was doing. We cannot understand why bad things happen to good people. We can only look to Him and ask for wisdom and guidance that can only be described as supernatural. During the course of the tragic events, Job was true to the Word of God and never cursed the God of Abraham, Jacob, or Isaac, and came away with a deeper understanding of a sovereign and just God.

Job approached bereavement in a very different manner than what most of us would. In verse 21, we discover that Job worshiped God. When the people who mean most to us are taken away, do we truly worship God, or do we merely go on and let our hearts bleed with emotional pain?

How do we prepare for the kinds of tragedies of life that plagued Job and our fictional character, Dick Sterling?

How is it possible to worship God during times of great loss?

The first chapter of Job includes a dialogue between Satan and God. Was it Satan who won the argument because God allowed him to bring ruin on Job? Does God give Satan power to bring havoc to our lives?

Take a few snapshots of your own. For example, the reaction of Job's wife, the type of anguish that job endured, and the kind of counsel that Job could have used are all topics within the context of a person in great need.

Day 36: Oneness in Onesimus

Scripture: Philemon 1:1 to 1:25

The historical record of our country is blemished with the crime of slavery. Several documentaries illustrate the great sin committed by humanity against an entire continent of people. Several years ago we watched the movie, "Roots" that dealt with a black man who tried to trace his heritage back to Africa. Our true roots as Christians are not in the sinful nature of this world but in our Creator. Still, we have obligations to others who are our superiors, and though we do not call them our "masters" we realize that there is a boss-employee code of interaction. Paul's short letter to Philemon provides instruction on how people change rolls as they become brothers and sisters in Christ. Philemon is a short account about a man named Onesimus who was a literal slave. As a free man, he returned to his "master" to become a coworker and spiritual servant for Jesus.

Focus Scripture: Philemon 1:7

"For I have come to have so much joy and comfort in your love, because the hearts of the saints have been refreshed through you, brother."

Focus Scripture: Philemon 1:15,16

"For perhaps he was for this reason parted from you for a while so that you may have him back forever, no longer as a slave, but more than a slave, a beloved brother especially to me, but how much more to you, both in the flesh and in the Lord."

Paul's Epistle to Philemon has some striking parallels to our pre-Christian conversion, our acceptance of Christ, and our total commitment to God's will. We go from being slaves after our own desires to becoming children of God, to becoming servants, desiring that the gospel be fulfilled in our homes, at school, and at our jobs. Onesimus may have carried Paul's letter to Philemon in Colossae where Onesimus was a run-away slave. According to Roman law he could have been executed on the spot. I think Philemon looked up over the letter at Onesimus (who may have had his head bowed) and he hugged him and said, "welcome home, brother. It's is good to see you." But, maybe there was a lag in time before forgiveness was granted.

Our gospel spread, first to the Jew, and then to the gentiles. Then the gospel became trans-cultural, trans-economic, and trans-racial so that today we almost lose sight of the first message that God's chosen people were the vehicle of Christianity. We all share a heritage with Onesimus in that we are slaves to this body and in great need to be accepted by God and others who similarly declare one Master over us and the Universe.

Compare the redemption plan of Christ with the acceptance of Onesimus. Are there any parallels?

How might Onesimus have been effective in his ministry?

What kind of situation may have occurred that Onesimus was converted to Christianity?

Day 37: Poetry, prophecy, and promises

Scripture – Psalms 1 – 3

Some time ago my wife, Susan, told me about a sparrow that flew into the window on the back side of our house. Motionless, the bird lie there, and it made Susan sad, seeing the eyes open but staring off into space. She covered the bird with a cloth and talked to God a while about the bird and shed a few tears at the sight of the pretty creature. Then, without any warning, the cloth moved and the bird thrashed the material aside and flew away. Susan looked on with great joy, such joy that she cried again. There was great poetry in the entire event and parallels to the death and resurrection. The parallels were so vivid and the message so personal to Susan, that she was overcome by emotion.

Psalms are that way. The verses reference actual events but they also are prophetic with ample use of metaphors and similes. When we read Psalms we will find that we identify with the verses, sometimes to the point that tears well up in our eyes, for we know that the Holy Spirit is causing us to take a snapshot of our lives and spirituality. The first three Psalms do well to exemplify the nature of the entire Book of Psalms, addressing issues of obedience to the Law of God, seeking and worshipping our Lord, and walking intensely with Him.

Focus Scripture: Psalms 1: 2, 3

> "But his delight is in the law of the Lord, and in His law he meditates day and night. And he will be like a tree firmly planted by streams of water."

Focus Scripture: Psalms 2:7, 8

> "I surely tell of the decree: The Lord said to me, 'You are my Son; today I have begotten you. Ask of me, and I will make the nations your heritage, and the ends of the earth your possession.'"

Focus Scripture: Psalms 2:12

> "Do homage to the Son, lest He become angry, and you perish in the way, for His wrath may soon be kindled. How blessed are all who take refuge in Him."

Focus Scripture: Psalms 3:7

> "Arise, O Lord; save me, O my God! For Thou hast smitten all my enemies on the cheek; Thou has shattered the teeth of the wicked."

At any moment in time we see a world that is in turmoil. Russia struggles with democracy while China struggles with a new kind of capitalistic communism. Millions have died in Somalia and other African countries at the hands of neighboring tribes. Iran and North Korean are well on their ways, or maybe already have nuclear weapons. There never seems to be lasting peace between Israel and her neighbors. The "teeth of the wicked" are clinched and wickedness appears to have won the first battle. In addition, the concept of "family" is being re-defined by people who never experienced the firm foundation of a family as defined by God.

To be sure, there is nothing more consistent than the Law of God and it is appropriate that Psalm 1 deals with this subject. Without the rules set down the plan for live cannot be lived with fulfillment and joy. The second Psalm is a prophesy of Christ and even states that through this Messianic prophecy all of humankind will be able to take refuge. Clearly, God has made a provision for the forgiveness of sins that we are all guilty of. Psalms 3 is a prayer, asking for continued salvation and protection as we charter the course of life.

> Oh, bird that goes awry in flight
> And is deceived by window glass
> You fall from glory, stately heights
> To earth as this day quickly passed.
>
> But then in glory you awoke
> And flew again to higher skies
> For iron death and chains are broke
> And God has stung the prince of lies.

You see, our snapshot of Psalms 1, 2, and 3 is blended with my own life and causes me to write another poem in order to canvass the great message that awaits those who plunge into the Psalms.

What other snapshots to you observe that are personal to you in these Psalms?

Try to find parallels that demonstrate what God is like; record them and revisit your illustrations after reading through these first three Psalms a second or third time.

Day 38: New Old Testament

Scripture - Hebrew 1:1 to 2:4

While we were living in Nigeria, my wife bought two water color paintings from a local artist. The subjects of the paintings were two African women, one carrying a vase on her head and the other smiling. These paintings captured a portion of Nigeria that we will never forget but it was not until Susan had them matted and framed that we fully appreciated the treasure that we now enjoy daily. The boarder and frame seem to tie the paintings together, almost like book ends. The colors leap out at us and the smile makes us smile back as we relate to our four years in Nigeria.

Hebrews is a book that seems to frame in the essence of the Bible, Old and New Testament. Many portions of this book use scripture reference to the Old Testament, helping to bring out the true spiritual truths that God intended for us. Instead of the OT being "old" in the sense that it is outdated, Hebrews emphasizes how it is new every day and applicable to our lives.

The universe is passing away and one day the pictures on our wall will decay. As we gaze into the vastness of the night time sky, we see a universe that has a beginning and has an end. We live in a wavelength of time and we grasp for things to make life purposeful. We cling to the past and hope for a future and that is exactly what the unknown author of Hebrews accomplishes in this amazing book.

Focus Scripture: Hebrews 1: 1-2

"God, after He spoke long ago to the fathers in the prophets in many portions and in many ways, in these last days has spoken to us in His Son, whom He appointed heir of all things, through whom also He made the world."

Focus Scripture: Hebrews 1:5 (from Psalm 2: 7)

"For to which of the angels did He ever say, 'Thou art My Son, today I have begotten thee?' And again, 'I will be a Father to Him and He shall be a son to Me.'"

Focus Scripture: Hebrews 1:10-11 (from Psalms: 102:25-26)

"And, Thou, Lord, in the beginning did lay the foundation of the earth, and the heavens are the works of thy hands; they will perish, but you remain..."

Focus Scripture: Hebrews 2: 3-4

"How shall we escape if we neglect so great a salvation? After it was first spoken through the Lord, it was confirmed to us by those who heard, God also bearing witness with them, both by signs and wonders and by various miracles and by gifts of the Holy Spirit according to His own will."

Although the universe is grinding down, the painting that God has given us is one of eternal life. We can rejoice that God is unchanging and He smiles at us daily, reminding us of where we have been and where we are going, reminding us that He created everything, so we need not be concerned about the perishable. And He did all this out of love. Even the angels are there to minister to us and help us through times of darkness, when there seems to be no way out of our circumstances, no way out of our physical and emotional pain.

It would seem hard to "neglect so great a salvation." But, we do so every day. There are times when we need to take an inventory of our daily activities and ask ourselves whether we are neglecting the One who made us, unique, creative, and loving. Then we should reflect on the snapshot that spans a time that is much more vast than our years on this planet.

Write a letter to someone and tell them what they mean to you and how thankful that you are that God has put them in your life.

In what specific ways do we neglect our salvation?

Is there a way that your life seems incomplete and "unframed?" What means are you using to change that situation?

What qualities do you see in the author of Hebrews?

Day 39: A wise man will hear

Scripture - Proverbs 1:1-33

As an undeclared premed major, I recall taking one of the most difficult biology classes that I ever attempted. At the same time, I was participating in un-wise activities. The day before an important test it was clear that additional "wisdom" was key, so I prayed for it. Certainly God would come through with the wisdom that I needed. I was asking God for wisdom on the day of testing but not on other days.

Focus scripture: Proverbs 1:5

"A wise man will hear, and will increase learning; and a man of understanding shall attain unto wise counsels..."

Focus scripture: Proverbs 1:28, 29

"They shall call upon me but I will not answer; they shall seek me but I will not answer; they shall seek me early but they shall not find me; because they hated knowledge, and did not choose the fear of the Lord."

I was a Christian trying to live out both lives of a believer and an unbeliever. I thought that I could carry God around like a pocket calculator (or slide rule, in those days). I got the lowest grade in the class on the exam even though I prayed. I failed first to choose the fear of the Lord and then seek knowledge and understanding as an outgrowth of that healthy fear. It was not until some years later that I realized what I was doing. My salvation was sealed but my prayers were selfish, directed at God to bail me out of trouble. If He had answered my prayer by letting me do well on the test, I would have done more self-destructive things because I would have banked on "God my good buddy" to come to the rescue. Fact of the matter is, He does bail me out on a regular basis but it is only because I continuously seek Him and earnestly pray for guidance. I have learned that God is not a spare tire but He is the entire vehicle. But, unlike a new car that wares out and becomes less dependable, this Vehicle becomes more comfortable and more powerful with every tank-full of prayer, praise, and worship.

If our lives are aligned toward God, our family, others, and our work, where should our prayer for wisdom be directed?

How should we pray during times when there does not appear to be any obvious fork in the road?

How should we pray when there is an obvious fork in the road?

Day 40: Honing the steel

Scripture – James 1: 1-21

Note that the lesson of Day 39, found in Proverbs, is strikingly similar in the Book of James. Both books commence with a practical guide to seeking wisdom. James emphasizes consistency and stability in the Christian in order to realize complete happiness and well being.

There was a good movie about a young man who entered a dog sled race in order to save the family farm. Against all odds the young man keeps going to finish the 500 mile race from Winnipeg to St. Paul, Minnesota. It was a story of endurance but also a story about reaching for strength when there was not any left in the cupboard. We see these kind of heroes daily and we sometimes don't even know it. They are the people with multiple sclerosis, severe depression, cancer; people that have lost everything that they own because of unexpected tragedy in their lives. Yet, they keep going. Some of them are Christians; many are not. I have never been in a situation where my faith has caused me to be confronted with life threatening trials but the author of James knew people who were in impossible positions, far worse than most of us have had to experience. Through it all, they had the enduring quality of endurance.

Focus Scripture: James 1:4

"...And let endurance have its perfect result, that you may be perfect and complete, lacking in nothing. But if any of you lacks wisdom, let him ask of God, who gives to all men generously and without reproach, and it will be given to him. But let him ask in faith without any doubting, for the one who doubts is like the surf of the sea driven and tossed by the wind."

Focus Scripture: James 1:12

"Blessed is a man who perseveres under trial, because when he has stood the test, he will receive the crown of life that God has promised to those who love him."

Focus Scripture: James 1:21

"Therefore putting aside all filthiness and all that remains of the wickedness, in humility receive the word implanted, which is able to save your souls."

The author, probably the half-brother of Jesus, is sewing together virtues of endurance, wisdom, faith, and living a pure life. If we have endurance but the endurance is selfserving, even it withers and fades. If we want endurance but lack wisdom we can ask God for it and expect an answer. If we lack faith, but would like to have faith, He will give us that too. But there is a "stipulation". We must try to live a pure and upright life, beyond reproach of others. Sometimes this is not easy but God knows when we try. The sled dog musher's name became "Ironwill" because he did not give up but the motive was not for himself but for his deceased father and his mother. If our motives are focused on high virtues, we too will finish the race and be real winners.

There must be a goal line or objective in mind every day when we get up. This goal is emphasized repeatedly in scripture and it is to serve others and meet their needs. We have written for us the ultimate social services program, calling us to direct our "iron will" toward feeding the hungry, visiting prisoners, taking care of the homeless, and sacrificially giving of ourselves. This servitude may be a plate of cookies for someone new in the neighborhood, sending a short note to someone we do not know very well, or giving away a used car. The list of possibilities is endless but the point is that our enduring qualities are directed to serving others. In the end we will genuinely feel God's presence in our lives.

What conclusions can we make when we see the same themes repeated several times in our Bible?

What does it mean to "receive the word implanted?"

Day 41: Discovered uncovered

Scripture - Ecclesiastes 1: 118

When I look under the hood of a 1970, American made automobile, I can describe the function of each part of the engine. When I look under the hood of an automobile that is newer than 1995, I am not sure of anything but the engine block. But, contrary to what diehard, old car owners may say, newer cars are better. They are more fuel efficient, safer, and they last longer than earlier vintages but there is one thing that has not fundamentally changed--the internal combustion engine. In one sense, there is nothing "new" about cars or any gasoline engine. The right mixture of gas and oxygen must be in the cylinder at the right time in order for an explosion to move the piston. All the gizmos such as fuel injection, computer modules, and electron ignition are just additives of the same old internal combustion engine. The author of Ecclesiastes was at a point in his life when he realized that all of our efforts to chase after the pleasures and wisdom of this world will end the same way. The engine of life runs the same way and the only thing certain is that every thing new becomes old and worn out.

Focus Scripture: Ecclesiastes 1:6

"Blowing toward the south, then turning toward the north, the wind continues swirling along; and on its circular courses the wind returns."

Focus Scripture: Ecclesiastes 1:10

> "Is there anything of which one might say, 'see this, it is new?' Already it has existed for ages which were before us."

Focus Scripture: Ecclesiastes 1:17

> "And I set my mind to know wisdom and to know madness and folly; I realized that this also is striving after wind."

Focus Scripture: Ecclesiastes 7: 14 (Jumping ahead with a "snapshot")

> "Enjoy prosperity while you can. But when hard times strike, realize that both come from God. That way you will realize that nothing is certain in this life."

When we read "scientists have discovered ..." this really means that something has been revealed to them. Astronomers looking at photographs from the Hubble telescope are finding out new things but they have not discovered anything. They have just uncovered what was known to God since He created this knowledge. The example of wind in verse 6 exemplifies this. Differential pressure on the earth's surface causes air masses to compensate and the wind blows around high or low pressure systems.

The author of Ecclesiastes expands the concept of acquiring "knowledge" in subsequent chapters. If our motivating drive is to obtain knowledge so that we can promote our selves above others, this too is all folly because we will wear ourselves out, never experiencing genuine happiness. If we direct our efforts to obtain knowledge to help others, that is an entirely different virtue.

What can be said for certain is that Jesus is the "new wine" that gives us hope in dealing with age-old problems. He reveals Himself to us every day and makes the machinery or purpose of life meaningful. Our challenge is to spread the good news of His ultimate sacrifice in an undeserving world. Every day should make us want to spend our time contemplating how we can use the tools of old for the purpose of a new day. Regardless of what the new day may bring, we must always recognize the sovereignty of a just and righteous God at the cog of the universe.

Ironically, when we read scripture, we tend to think that we discovered something significant when, in fact, we have been shown a truth that applies to us in a personal and life-changing manner. The more often we take snapshots of our Bible, the more often we tune our spiritual engines and grease the gears of experience with the anointing oil of God's goodness.

Think of some technology that you have become aware of and evaluate the "newness" of it. What former concept went into the invention?

Now think about what present day things make you truly happy. What spiritual truth lies within the happiness that you feel?

How do we keep zeal for living a part of us when "there is nothing new under the sun?"

Complete this statement: We cannot control how the wind blows but we can control how we _____ _____.

Day 42: Not from around here?

Scripture - 1 Peter 1:125

When our family moved to Canada we found that we were somewhat alienated by a different work place, school, and community. I remember being in a restaurant where my wife asked for some ice in her water and the waiter looked at her like she was from outer space...an alien from the United States. People moving from Canada to Houston are even more alienated than we were. We never lost our identity as Americans while in Canada and neither will a Canadian who works in the U.S. Similarly, Peter reminds us that as creatures of the Spirit, we are just passing through. It was necessary for Paul to write this letter as many converted Jews were being driven out of Jerusalem, families were split up, people needed to pack up and move their vocations to different regions. As a result, Christianity expanded. We are also asked to "move on" and take on different rolls in our community and impact the people around us.

Every once in a while a movie is released that depicts an extraterrestrial coming to earth on a mission but having trouble returning to their home. The director of the movie wants us to identify with the creature's predicament through our own experiences so that we think to ourselves "poor little alien, I hope it can find a way off this planet and go home." In Peter's first epistle he refers to some Christians as "aliens," meaning that they are not in a native setting.

151

Focus Scripture: 1 Peter 1: 34

> "Blessed be the God and Father of our Lord Jesus Christ, who according to His great mercy has caused us to be born again to a living hope through the resurrection of Jesus Christ from the dead, to obtain an inheritance which is imperishable and undefiled and will not fade away, reserved in heaven for you."

Focus Scripture: 1 Peter 1: 14-16 (Living Bible)

> "Obey God because you are his children; don't slip back into your old ways – doing evil because you knew not better. But be holy now in everything you do, just as the Lord is holy, who invited you to be his child. He himself has said, 'you must be holy, for I am holy.'"

Focus Scripture: 1 Peter 1: 2223

> "Since you have in obedience to the truth purified your souls for a sincere love of the brethren, fervently love one another from the heart, for you have been born again not of seed which is perishable but imperishable, that is, through the living and abiding word of God."

Peter mentions twice in this chapter the concept and reality of being "born again." Being born again means that we have a whole different heritage as compared to our human kinship. Being born again (from a Spirit that is not from this world) we qualify as legal aliens. This old perishable world and everything in it is a foreign place to us. We have a right to be here but we are also burdened with an ambassadorship. Now, we belong to a genuinely extraterrestrial, heavenly family. We are asked to sow this seed that is also imperishable and will not rot in the ground. We are asked to love one another so that the whole world can see that we are really aliens, on a mission to rescue the people of this planet. The task at hand is to present ourselves to others as genuine so that we are not asked to return to our own "planet" of "religion."

Are we asking others to become aliens in a familiar land when we share our gospel with them?

If the above is true, then what roll does the Holy Spirit play in our testimony to others?

What trials tested the faith of early Christians, as compared to trials in Western society?

How do we get people to ask directions when they feel comfortable with where they are going?

Chapter 1 of 1 Peter has several truths and guidelines for living a meaningful life, not just for ourselves but for our Lord. Read through the chapter and record your own snapshots about living a testimony with bold ambassadorship.

Day 43: Get a sitter

Scripture: Songs of Solomon: Chapters 1-2

After many years of reading this scripture, I have come to the conclusion that this book is truly the most unusual book in the entire Bible. Songs of Solomon is a book that deals with love in perspective, not just the warm feelings that we have for one another, but this book deals with the flaming hot issues of sex and inner beauty. To those who think that Christians are prudes that never let themselves go, this is the romance of humankind between husband and wife. Every man should identify the writing as a description of their beautiful wife; every wife should see their own husband in these poetic descriptions.

Focus Scripture: Songs of Solomon: 1:12-14 (The Shulamite)

> "While the King was at his table, my perfume spread its fragrance. My lover is to me a sachet of myrrh resting between my breasts. My lover is to me a cluster of henna blossoms from the vineyards of En Gedi."

Focus Scripture: Songs of Solomon: 2:1-2

> "I am a rose of Sharon, a lily of the valleys. Like a lily among thorns is my darling among the maidens"

Some commentaries declare that one purpose of this book is to show the parallels between Christ and His Bridegroom, the Church. If one feels that interpretation is true, it must come from the Holy Spirit. But to me, the book is an important piece of evidence that God really does more than just exist. He has made undefiled love a very real experience and not just a sexual interlude.

I feel that every word written in this book is about my wife. But it is also written for every wife and every husband. There is nothing more wonderful than being with her all of the time whether we are sexually expressing this love or just holding hands and clinging to a precious moment of time. Just as a beautiful lake, mantled by towering pines is evidence that God is the creator of the material world, my wife shows me the real breath of life that He breathed into all of us.

If you have married the love of your life, how does beauty manifest itself? If not married, what will be the qualities of the opposite other that will make he or she unique?

How would Solomon view commercialization of beauty of the 21st century?

Day 44: Bolt "A" in hole "B"

Scripture II Peter 1:121

When my children were very young we purchased a swing set. A demonstration model was set up in front of the store where it was purchased and the kids were elated that they were about to have a swing set exactly like the one in front of the store. In their minds, some man would come out to our house and unload this beautiful toy and they would be playing on it within three seconds. They were somewhat disappointed that the swing set would have to be assembled by Daddy. "Oh well, Daddy can do that in about 30 seconds and then we will play for the rest of the day." Little did they know that Daddy would sacrifice that weekend in order to assemble their new entertainment system. There were about 90 screws and bolts, no two looking alike. But, the little gymnasium of the yard was slowly erected until it was time to mount the various swings on the frame. None of the screws were long enough to assemble the remaining swing set. I looked down at the instructions as several drops of sweat came rolling down my nose and splattered on the instructions (written in five different languages). I realized that I needed the very bolts that were just slightly too long which were ferociously snug in the frame. The kids had long since gone over to the neighbor's house to play because Daddy, even with his Masters degree, could not put together a swing set. Come Sunday evening, the engineering marvel was finally completed, but not until I disassembled part of it, reread the instructions, visited the display model at the store, and carefully selected the right bolt for each part of the yard gym. It was a frustrating experience but I can confidently say that if

I ever have to assemble that particular model swing set again, I will have it done in less than twelve hours.

Peter talks about reading instructions and paying close attention as to how our salvation and how our effectiveness as Christians is manifest. He is the one who bought the swing set but he also is one of the people who saw the fundamental framework of our salvation, Jesus Christ. He is an expert but he also knows how frustrating it is to follow instructions. Nevertheless, he encourages us to never give up. Peter further warns us (especially in Chapter 2) that we can be influenced by the wrong people or things of this world.

Focus Scripture: II Peter 1:1011

> "Therefore brethren, be all the more diligent to make certain about His calling and choosing you; for as long as you practice these things, you will never stumble; for in this way the entrance into the eternal kingdom of our Lord and Savior Jesus Christ will be abundantly supplied to you."

Focus Scripture: II Peter 1:2021

> "But know this first of all, that no prophecy of Scripture is a matter of one's own interpretation, for no prophecy was ever made by an act of human will, but men moved by the Holy Spirit spoke from God."

The biblical prophecies all made very good sense to Peter...at least at the time when he wrote this letter to a small but growing congregation. This Peter is probably the same Peter who denied Christ three times before the Lord was crucified. But now he knows that the entrance to the Kingdom of God will be more meaningful to believers in their attempt to help others assemble a spiritual swing set. God, of course, is the manufacturer, and we will make mistakes, but He knows that, because we keep on trying, we will become more effective Christians, one bolt at a time.

It doesn't do any good to dwell on what we did wrong or to dwell on our difficult circumstances as Christians. The neighbors may even laugh at us as we try to assemble the swing set but the neighborhood kids may end up playing on it and realize that Jesus is, after all, the only way to true fulfillment. But we are not just set loose with the instruction manual (our Bibles); we are given the Holy Spirit who will offer guidance when selecting the right spiritual tool.

Think of something that you assembled wrong and write a parallel on how the assembly worked out or was corrected.

Peter talks about "cleverly invented stories" in verse 16. Site some examples of how this present world tried to de-rail our efforts as Christians.

Day 45: Good guy in black hat

Scripture: Isaiah 1:131

Western movie satires and skits are funny in a groaning kind of way. These satires are like the melodramas of silent movies when the Canadian police rescues the young maiden who is tied to the railroad tracks because she vows never to marry the vile character. The hero in the western satire always wears a hat that is too big and walks with sway from side to side, as if his horse were still beneath him. When the slimy outlaw arrives in town, everyone disappears except the hero in the white hat. If the melodrama is overtly satirized, the facade of store fronts fall over, revealing the Hollywood backdrop. Suddenly the viewer is laughing at the camera crew and the offstage actors. This usually occurs near the end of the comedy, after the plot has fully developed. We laugh at the outrageous climax to a satire that was never meant to be believable. We no longer think of the characters as credible but know that everything is a farce.

Focus Scripture: Isaiah 1:2-3

> "Hear, O heavens! Listen, O earth! For the Lord has spoken; 'I reared children and brought them up, but they have rebelled against me. The ox knows his master, the donkey his owner's manger, but Israel does not know, my people do not understand.'"

Focus Scripture: Isaiah 1:11

> "To what purpose is the multitude of your sacrifices into me? saith the Lord; I am full of burnt offerings of rams, and the fat of fed beasts and I delight not in the blood of bullocks, or of lambs, or hegoats."

Focus Scripture: Isaiah 1:27,28a

> "Zion will be redeemed with justice, and her repentant ones with righteousness. But transgressors and sinners will be crushed together."

Just as the viewer of the western satire can readily see the ridiculous and phony characterizations, so can God recognize insincere efforts to worship him. The irony of salvation is that the good guy in the white hat is not always the one who is saved from damnation. God sees right through the facade, the false set. He sees the genuine followers. Sometimes the genuine believers do not even look like the "good guys."

When Jesus was here on earth, He did not deliberately seek the religious crowd. Instead we find Jesus with the outcasts who have come to a point of spiritual impoverishment. He proclaims, "Blessed be the poor in spirit, for theirs is the Kingdom of heaven (Matthew 5:3)." But those who cast off the feeling of self-sufficiency and allow God to expose their false possessions will be brought into the realm of lasting security.

As the Western satire closes, everyone looks pretty silly. We like to see the good guy win. We realize that the play or movie was all in good fun and that there was no real genuine story being told. If our lives are lived this way, the comedy becomes a tragedy because the things of this world and the prince of darkness were allowed to divert our attention away from a Holy God. Conversely, if we sacrifice our hearts and thoughts to God, we will feel fulfillment as the curtain is drawn in the last act of our lives.

Are there areas of our personal lives that should be exposed to ridicule?

Isaiah writes in verse 30, "You will be like an oak with fading leaves, like a garden without water." What application might these words have for us?

If you were to compare the scripture of Day 43 (II Peter) to the words of Isaiah, how are the warnings similar?

Without recording your thoughts on paper, how can you correct a bad situation that is a result of unrighteous living? Record them in your heart.

Day 46: There's the light!

Scripture: 1 John: 1:1 to 2:14

It was a beautiful evening on Eagles Nest Lake. Aside from not catching any fish, it was perfect. The lake was like transparent velvet and as the sun started it's decent into the pine mantled horizon, all I could think about was the walleye that would have no choice than to smack my drifting minnow. There is a steel shaft of stubbornness that supports the spine of every fisherman, and I was going to find that fish this evening. But darkness set in and the moon was not shining that night, and utter blackness set in very quickly. I was not very familiar with the lake but was pretty certain that if I headed west, I would find my way back to the cabin I was renting. Suddenly I realized that I was motoring my boat into one of many bays around the lake. I was lost and the blue velvet waters turned to the same slate color as the cloud filled sky. I was not so confident as before that I knew where West was. Finally, I took the boat to what I thought to be the middle of the lake and squinted to see a light. With a prayer, I found a single porch light on the far shore. It was with great rejoicing that I made it home where I should have been. I had lost my sense of direction; my point of reference.

Focus Scripture: 1 John: 1:3

> "What we have seen and heard we proclaim to you also, that you also may have fellowship with us; and indeed our fellowship is with the Father, and with His Son, Jesus Christ."

Earl Fashbaugh

Focus Scripture: 1 John: 2:3

> "And by this we know that we have come to know Him, if we keep His commandments."

Focus Scripture: 1 John: 2:11

> "But the one who hates his brother is in the darkness and walks in the darkness, and does not know where he is going because the darkness has blinded his eyes."

John seems to scramble various themes in the first two chapters of 1 John. First he talks about fellowship and Christ's sacrifice, then he talks about forgiveness and keeping His commandments, and finally John deals with the interpersonal relationships that confront us daily. At first glance, the concepts seem incoherent but actually the author, John, has knitted a very warm garment called Christian living. He emphasizes the focal point of our salvation, the Light, the sacrifice, and then takes this joy through a full circle and explains that there is no room in our hearts for bitterness, jealousy, or haughtiness. If we focus back on the Christ who loves us, we internalize the message that severs us from selfish bondage.

It was a scary feeling to be out on a dark lake, not knowing the exact direction to go. At first, I entered a large bay, which should have been named "Sucker Bay." As Christians, we sometimes attempt to look to these dark-bay alternatives when dealing with others and then try to pretend that we are in the Light. Our own solutions to interpersonal conflicts are usually contrary to what God has intended. He would prefer that we go to the center of the lake and look for the true Light, because our own intuition will often lead us even further into "Sucker Bay."

In verses 2:12-14 John refers to his readers as "dear children, fathers, and young men." What level of spiritual maturity are you at and why?

John was very old when he wrote these words. What underlying concern do you think was bothering him when John wrote this book? How may these concerns be relevant, today?

Take a snapshot of a situation in your life and how you found a point of reference that transformed you from feeling lost to being found.

How can you recognize deception?

Day 47: Put words in my mouth

Scripture: Jeremiah 1:1 to 1:19

We have all heard the expression, "don't put words in my mouth." The expression may have come from this scripture. The Word from God is that He will put words into Jeremiah's mouth for the sake of a spiritually sick nation. At the time that God declared Jeremiah His chosen prophet, he was just a boy, but God told him that He knew Jeremiah before he was born, before he was conceived.

My wife and I can relate to this. Before our son, Jonathan, was born we imagined him and we loved him very much. When I look at Jon at the supper table I think about the promise that God placed in our hearts. In fact, when we were trying to decide on a name for him, Jonathan stuck on our tongues and there was no other name that we could imagine. There are at least two messages in this portion of scripture: first, the sacred destination of the unborn, and second, a need for a decaying people to repent before God revokes His continuous protection.

Focus Scripture: Jeremiah 1:5

"Before I formed you in the womb, I knew you, and before you were born, I consecrated you."

Focus Scripture: Jeremiah 1:7

> "But the Lord said to me, 'Do not say, "I am only a child." You must go to everyone I send you to and say whatever I command you. Do not be afraid of them, for I am with you and will rescue you, declares the Lord.'"

Focus Scripture: Jeremiah 1:12

> "Then the Lord said to me, 'you have seen well, for I am watching over my word to perform it.'"

Focus Scripture: Jeremiah 1:19

> "And they will fight against you, but they will not overcome you, for I am with you to deliver you, 'declares the Lord.'"

We can imagine the scorn that Jeremiah was subject to. He was merely a youth when God's declaration came to him. For the next forty years he would carry a message of doom to Israel because they turned aside from the God that delivered them from bondage. Israel is about to go into another kind of bondage, both political and spiritual. A kid was going to tell them so. But God was not just putting words into Jeremiah's mouth. God was commanding Jeremiah to look to the Word of God which is compared to an almond rod in verse 12. We can take great solace that, if God will help Jeremiah, He will also help us when we stand up against decaying moral attitudes and people who try to remove God from our country.

Whether young or old, we have certain talents and levels of maturity. But, if we examine our own powers, we will feel inadequate in the area of witnessing to others. Spiritual decay can progress to a point where we ignore immorality and even indulge in impurity. Either we turn the wheel forward, and realize that we must be adequate or God would not have put us in any given situation, or we look at the face value of our own abilities and miss the opportunity to blow a whistle or say something to someone about our beliefs.

When a professional baseball player faces a tough fastball pitcher, he does not say to himself, "I better not swing at this fastball because I do not think I am quick enough to hit this pitch." Instead he says, "I recognize this fastball and am going to swing at it because it is coming right over the plate." So it is with our ability to recognize great opportunities to witness and use our situation as God intended.

An example comes to mind concerning my father-in-law, who is currently in a nursing home. Although his short-term memory is not what it used to be, he is quick to tell others that God loves them and that he will pray for them. Then he follows through and commits his prayers for those that have not made peace with God and are quickly running out of time. He makes a conscious decision to take his present situation and share what he knows about the Love of God rather than slump back in a chair and wait for the inevitable.

Ironically, Jeremiah never saw the people of Judah heed his words. He spent 40 years warning a nation about destruction but they did not change their ways. It did not matter because Jeremiah followed through and acted in obedience, leaving the rest to God. At times, it seems futile to mention Godly things to the ungodly but it is not ours to see the outcome of our own witness—at least not now.

What does Jeremiah 1:5 mean when referring to being known before being formed in the womb?

How can we feel a purpose in life if we cannot see the results of our good works?

How can we continue doing the right thing if we do not have a purpose?

Does serving God guarantee our physical well being? How and how not?

Day 48: Tell me the Truth

Scripture: II John: 1-13

When my son was in elementary school, he had a friend overnight; the two boys stayed in a tent in the back yard. It all seemed like a perfectly innocent plan until we found out the next day that several other boys were having sleep-overs with a master minded plan to sneak out and carouse the neighborhood. Abbreviating the story, Susan caught Jonathan returning home. He brought with him a fragmental story about how a strange looking man started to chase the boys down the block and how his friend went straight home. We knew we weren't given the whole story. The next day Susan got quite a different version from a police officer who was given Jonathan's name as an associate involved in a crime. It seems that one of the boys reached into the back seat of a parked car, took a soccer ball out and kicked it down the street. The perfect stranger who chased the boys was a retired police officer – an entirely different story than the one we got. In Jon's mind, he did not lie, he just....well....left out some of the truth.

Focus Scripture: II John: 7-9

"For many deceivers have gone out into the world, those who do not acknowledge Jesus Christ as coming in the flesh. This is the deceiver and the antichrist. Watch yourselves, that you might not lose what we have accomplished, but that you may receive a full reward. Anyone who goes too far and does not abide in the teaching of Christ, does not have God; the one who abides in the teaching, he has both the Father and the Son."

The best thing that could have happened to the boys is that they got caught. In fact, if one of them had not taken the soccer ball out of the car, there might not be any lesson at all for my son. Unfortunately, many kids do not get caught and they continue to take the deceiving path right into the court room and to jail. More unfortunate, is the group of religious people who take part of the story of Jesus and apply it to their own religion. They have done what my son tried to do, and give the story a different twist. The Bible says to be wary of anyone who distorts the Truth. We do not have to hold up a shield against them but we must be ready to share the whole gospel message and not leave out the detail, like He arose from a state of death after three days.

I am very proud of my son because he has developed into a God-fearing husband who will not compromise the truth. He was vulnerable at one time but is a strong Christian now. As a boy, I came home with a few of my own stories where I just....well....left out some of the truth. Jon is not justified by my actions: he is justified and sanctified by the saving grace of Christ.

The apostle John was concerned that love and truth were not genuine in the early church. How is the situation similar or different today?

How are love and truth connected?

Day 49: Lamentations to lemonade

Scripture: Lamentations 1:1 to 2:2

To "Lament" means to grieve. We usually denote extreme grief when we refer to lamenting. Complete destruction had fallen on all of Israel. No longer were the busy Passover feasts, the preserved family life, grandpa passing on the words of comfort and wisdom to the children. The destruction was analogous to a huge forest fire burning everything beyond recognition.

There are two kinds of trees that do very well after forest fires. They are Jack Pines and Douglas Firs. Jack Pines are as much God's creation as Douglas Firs, but as far as aesthetics go, Jack Pines are ugly trees, while Douglas Firs are majestic and provide building materials. Both of these trees do well after fires because the seeds of the other trees are completely destroyed, but the cones of the Jack Pine and Douglas Fir pop open and seeds are liberated to grow without competition from other plants. In fact, these trees take nutrients left in the soft ashes after the forest fire.

Focus Scripture: Lamentations 1:1

> "How deserted lies the city once so full of people! How like a widow is she, who once was great among the nations! She that was queen among the provinces has now become a slave!"

Focus Scripture: Lamentations 1:8

> "Jerusalem has sinned greatly and so has become unclean. All who honored her despise her, for they have seen her nakedness; she herself groans and turns away."

Focus Scripture: Lamentations 2:5

> "The Lord was an enemy; He has swallowed up Israel. He has swallowed up all her palaces and destroyed her strongholds. He has multiplied mourning and lamentation for the Daughter of Judah."

Focus Scripture: Lamentations 2:8b

> "...therefore he made the rampart and the wall to lament; together they wasted away."

One study done on Minnesota forests revealed that there may be fewer than 6 Jack Pines per acre in a mature forest, but after a forest fire, there may be 15,000 to 20,000 seedlings (The Forest, Time Library, 1971). They may not be the loveliest tree, but they start the forest over again, as do the Douglas Firs in mountainous areas. The message of Lamentations is that sin has caused total destruction and God has given sinners over to their own destiny. Unfortunately, an entire society can fall. If there is one seed of hope that emulates from Lamentations (Chapter 3), it is that we must admit our sin to God, ask forgiveness, and know that we are forgiven.

After forgiveness comes growth. We then sink our roots into the "ashes" of our mistakes and experience unfettered renewal of our spirit. For at this level of turning around from sin, we lift our limbs high towards the "Son."

What do failed governments have in common?

How many families have been destroyed by alcoholism or unfaithfulness? Is the destruction gradual or sudden? Is destruction irreparable?

What has happened cannot be undone, any more than a forest fire. New life begins with the seeds of admission of sin and the forest is renewed. We all have examples of how new seeds germinate after a fire in our lives. Record some of the seeds in your life.

How can it be good to lament?

Verse 5 says, "The Lord is like an enemy." How can God be an "enemy" to His own?

How can we start over when we feel defeated?

Day 50: Dead beat Diotrephes

Scripture: III John

One beautiful Autumn day, my father and I put up some plastic on his back porch in order to keep the pending snow out. Some of the plastic was new and some of it had been used for a number of seasons. When winter did arrive, I checked on his place and the old plastic was totally shredded and unable to contain even a trace of precipitation. It would appear that when the weather turned cold, the old plastic lost all resilience. This makes me think of people who do not accept new missionaries, even though they bring fresh ideas and talents to the mission field. Some people have rigid ideas as to what constitutes a mission or missionary. They have trouble appreciating and supporting new material that protects the entire world and brings warmth to the great mission of evangelism, even in the coldest of historical times. The stubborn, resistant, and selfish do nothing but alienate the world with their flapping in the wind. They are like the shredded plastic.

This short letter discusses two contrasting and opposing church members, Gaius and Diotrephes. Gaius accepted authority and was ready to help further the gospel. Diotrephes fought against authority and spread vial words about the apostle, John.

Focus Scripture: III John: 1:3

> "It gave me great joy to have some brothers come and tell about your faithfulness to the truth and how you continue to walk in the truth. I have no greater joy than to hear that my children are walking in the truth."

Focus Scripture: III John: 1:5 (talking about Gaius)

> "Beloved, you are acting faithfully in whatever you accomplish for the brethren, and especially when they are strangers."

Focus Scripture: III John: 1;10 (talking about Diotrephes)

> "For this reason, if I come, I will call attention to his deeds which he does, unjustly accusing us with wicked words; and not satisfied with this, neither does he himself receive the brethren, and he forbids those who desire to do so, and puts them out of the church."

Gaius may have been pretty well off and gave of himself and his resources in order to keep the new missionaries coming and going. Today, he would be the guy who sponsors several young couples to third world missionaries and encourages them to come and visit and share their excitement. Diotrephes, if he were in contemporary settings, would be an elder of the First Church of the Dead Beats, where everyone stays in their protected circles.

I feel kind of sorry for Diotrephes. After all, he could have been a Christian but he was selfish with everything, including his financial resources. This would lead to utter depression and loneliness in old age. He would be like shredded plastic blown in the cold wind of old age, feeling useless, powerless, and maybe unlovable.

What is the underlying concern that John has when it comes to Christian conduct?

Looking back at the book of James he writes, "Do not merely listen to the word, and so deceive your selves. Do what it says. Anyone who listens to the word but does not do what it says is like a man who looks at his face in a mirror and, after looking at himself, goes away and immediately forgets what he looks like. But the man who looks intently into the perfect law that gives freedom, and continues to do this, not forgetting what he has heard, but doing it – he will be blessed in what he does (James 1: 22-25)." How do John and James emphasis genuine purpose and well-being in a Christian's life?

Speculate on how Gaius became the loving person and how Diotrephes became self centered. Do we start out like Gaius or do we start out like Diotrephes?

What gets in the way of Diotrephes becoming a genuine and accepted leader in the church?

How do we become leaders?

Day 51: You saw what?

Scripture: Ezekiel 1:1 to 2:3

Had Ezekiel written this book today, he most certainly would have been accused of overdosing on hallucinogens. Here is a man that saw a vision. Imagine the psychologist busy writing down the following:

Patient has seen the following vision:
- Four creatures that were of human form; all four have four faces.
- Each creature has four wings.
- Each has a hand under their wings.
- The four faces resemble the following: man, bull, lion, and eagle.
- When they moved, they mobilized on a single wheel that was full of eyes.
- Patient claims to have seen God above the four creatures.

Psychologist: Tell me Ezekiel, how old are you; and how long have you been seeing this "vision?"

Ezekiel: I am 30 years old and I have never seen a vision like this. I was taken up by the spirit of God and given a scroll and told to eat it.

Psychologist: Let's get this straight, God asked you to eat a scroll after you saw all of this ...err...vision?

Ezekiel: Yes, I have been sent to be a messenger for God and He showed me that there was a means for everyone to be redeemed by God. He showed me that salvation will be brought to all people who repent and turn to righteousness.

Psychologist: You seem to be a religious person. Is your religion important to you?

Ezekiel: Look, I am what God has made me. Phony religion will never give a person peace, but I am not here to talk about me, I am here to talk about you.

Psychologist: You mean you see visions and you don't think you need help? Then, why are you here? Explain why you want to talk about me.

Ezekiel: I am here to warn you that judgment and damnation are very real but that if you change your ways, and become reconciled with God, you can have joy and peace that are priceless.

Focus Scripture: Ezekiel 1:12

"And each went straight forward: wherever the spirit was about to go, they would go, without turning as they went."

Focus Scripture: Ezekiel 1:20

"Wherever the spirit was about to go, they would go in that direction. And the wheels rose close beside them; for the spirit of the living beings was in the wheels."

Focus Scripture: Ezekiel 2:1

"Then He said to me, 'Son of man, stand on your feet that I may speak to you!'"

One has to read the entire book of Ezekiel, perhaps a couple of times before the profound message has an impact. With time, the creatures described by Ezekiel make perfect sense. The eyes in the wheels make sense, the four faces of the four creatures make sense. Here is a message that has mobility and far reaching "vision." Ezekiel's message was not to his countrymen, the Jews. It was to the Babylonians, the very people that were holding him captive. The message given to Ezekiel is one of evangelism...very serious evangelism. Later on in the book, God tells Ezekiel that the blood of the condemned individual will be on his head if Ezekiel fails to get out the warning. God seems to be saying, "stand up and listen to me. Don't rest in your own righteousness. Open your mouth and let My word be known."

A common question that used to be asked is, "What do you have for wheels?" It may be more of a conversation piece among males than females but, the car we drive is often the center of discussion. As trivial as it seems, guys like to talk about cars because they are a part of American culture. We love to drive, go places, see people, and socialize. In a way, we match our vehicles with our mannerism. When Ezekiel wrote, "the spirit of the living beings was in the wheels" he was saying that the Word of God would be contained in the "vehicle" of the one who talked to others. The message would become the mannerism.

Does the Spirit of God, guide our wheels or do the wheels we drive guide our character? More importantly, do we ask God to be a passenger or do we ask Him to guide our wheels? We should all want to pray, "Lord, please forgive me for not letting the message leave my mouth. Thank you for guiding me. Thank you for another chance to deliver your message, today."

What message may we glean from the verse, "wherever the spirit was about to go, they would go?"

Earl Fashbaugh

How seriously should we take our personal responsibility to evangelize? Are we doing enough?

On Day 50 we looked at III John and saw a similar but different message dealing with evangelism. Is there a common denominator in these two portions of scripture?

Day 52: The cancer cure

Scripture: Jude: 1-25

Her name was Lindsey. Aside from a picture a mutual friend showed me, I did not know her, but I knew her mother, Lois. She was and is one of the most charming people I have ever known. Lindsey died of cancer. She was a pretty little girl who resembled her mother. The mysteries of God - can we ever understand them all in this life? No. If we could remove a cancer from a beautiful child without killing her, would we? Most certainly.

Many cancer researchers claim that we all have pre-cancerous potential in our bodies. Some of us have more of a genetic susceptibility to cancer than others. The trick to treating cancer is leaving the healthy cells alone, killing the cancerous cells, and perhaps getting the pre-cancerous cells to conform to a different genetic signal. The church was born by the death and resurrection of Christ but early in church history there were non-believers who infiltrated the congregations. They are like the potentially cancerous cells that can destroy the entire body unless the body recognizes them. Ideally, we have people in our church who come out of curiosity, people who are seriously seeking comfort and truth. If these "seekers" meet antagonistic members who only want to glorify themselves, they will leave and the cancerous members will become the cells of the dying church.

Focus Scripture: Jude 1:4

"For certain persons have crept in unnoticed, those who were long beforehand marked out for this condemnation, ungodly persons who turn the grace of our God into licentiousness (sensuality) and deny our only Master and Lord, Jesus Christ."

Focus Scripture: Jude 1:8

"Yet in the same manner these men. also by dreaming, defile the flesh and reject authority, and revile angelic majesties."

Focus Scripture: Jude 1:17

'But you must remember, beloved, the predictions of the apostles of our Lord Jesus Christ. They said to you, "In the last time there will be scoffers, following their own ungodly passions."'

Focus Scripture: Jude 1:22

"And have mercy on some, who are doubting; save others, snatching them out of the fire; and on some have mercy with fear, hating even the garment polluted by the flesh."

My old friend, Lois, will probably never read these words, but it must be stated that her daughter was not at fault for having the cancer. The cancer analogy is imperfect because we cannot control our genetic composition. It is very difficult to immediately recognize the members of the congregation that are out to destroy the unity of the Body of Christ. Most of the time, the people who look and smell the worst are the people who are in need of mercy and love, while there may be individuals who dress and carry themselves well, but they may be dangerous, cancer cells in the church. If these people are asked to take leadership rolls in the church, a cancer will develop, and division may take place unless the small tumor is immediately removed from the body.

If there were one person outside of my family who has influenced my spiritual conviction, I would have to declare that Pastor Leonard Anderson would rise to the top of the list. He was a leader in a church that Lois attended who caused me to look at the Word of God and put the rest of the world on trial. When we scrutinize the wisdom of this passing world next to Bible instruction we quickly find that many of the ideas of humankind are cancerous and cause us to drift away. I will never forget the day that Pastor Leonard placed in my hand a Living Bible to take off to college. That Bible is now pretty old and the outside is ugly but the inside contains the secrets of joyous living. In one of Pastor Leonard's sermons he told of a preacher who held up an Astronomy textbook and declared, "This book will show you how the heavens go." Then he held up a Bible and declared, "This book will show you how to go to Heaven."

That message must be the one that we cling to in our church, today. When we depart from the warnings and proclamations of God's Word we stray from the DNA of His Divine will. God could intervene any time and to tell the truth, I do not know why He does not. But, our choice to do His will as we were predestined to is exactly that—our decision. We decide on an individual scale and we decide as a body of believers who hold to the ultimate constitution—the Word of God.

What could Jude 1:8 be talking about when referring to "men, also by dreaming, defile the flesh and reject authority?"

The Church can be defiled by sinful behavior, but an analogy occurs in our own spiritual being. Are there "cancer cells" that we have to be aware of in our personal being?

What does the verse mean when referring to having mercy on those who have doubts?

What does "have mercy with fear" mean?

The best way to combat the disease, cancer, is to teach the body to somehow recognize the dangerous cells and teach them to multiply "normally." What analogy could be drawn about recognizing and treating unrighteousness in our church?

Day 53: A geologist's "fault"

Scripture: Daniel 1:1-21

One day in the lab at work an engineer and technician were testing the strength of a column of concrete. I became very excited when the concrete finally ruptured in the hydraulic vice. I proceeded to explain to my co-workers how exciting it was to see the concrete fracture at approximately 30 degrees from vertical. To me, the test replicated fault movement in the earth. The same day I talked to the engineer and he told me how just a little bit of clay or some other impurities in concrete has a dramatic effect on the strength. For obvious reasons, all major construction projects are subject to multiple concrete tests. Just as a few impurities in concrete can have a tragic impact on the building material - so it is with our spiritual composition: If we allow "little sins" in our normal life, the construction project suffers, and so does our testimony. Daniel was a young man who was tested and found to be much stronger (and wiser) than the others because he refused to take on the impure life style of the king and the others around him.

Focus Scripture: Daniel 1:8

"So Daniel made up his mind that he would not defile himself with the king's choice food or with the wine which he drank; so he sought permission from the commander of the officials that he might not defile himself."

Focus Scripture: Daniel 1:12

> "Please test your servants for ten days, and let us be given some vegetables to eat and water to drink."

Focus Scripture: Daniel 1:20

> "And as for every matter of wisdom and understanding about which the king consulted them, he found them ten times better than all the magicians and conjurers who were in all his realm."

We must never aspire to be the building block that sits high off the ground from the structure. Instead, we must ask to be good servants and present ourselves as good building material for the church. It took great courage for Daniel to deny a lifestyle, but in the end, he was a much better leader. Small sins have big consequences. The implications are that we cannot be fully utilized by our spiritual Bridge Builder unless we ask Him to remove the things that make us weak in the eyes of the rest of the world. We must make sure we are spiritually strong, so that when severe stress is applied, we will withstand the test without "fracturing." We can learn a lot from a young servant who aspired to stay pure and undefiled. Christ made a similar commitment on our behalf and rightfully takes on the ultimate leadership position.

Today, Daniel would have been offered rich foods, chips and salsa, high caloric Alfredo Sauce, and copious amounts of red wine. As we all know, this kind of food, with an abundance of fat and sugar, will eventually cause the pants to go asunder. But, more importantly, we get distracted from a healthy life style. The main point in Daniel, however, is that we must strive after purity. Do we do as well as Daniel? Maybe not, but we must put our priorities in order and try to present ourselves to the One King of Kings as worthy of duty.

How can we enhance our spiritual strength? How can we diminish our spiritual weakness and vulnerability?

When others see our strength, what related characteristics do they see in us?

Given that wine and certain meats were acceptable among the Jewish people, why was purity connected to drinking water and eating vegetables?

Day 54: To meet my bride

Scripture: Hosea, Chapters 1 and 2

I met Susan at an Intervarsity Christian Fellowship meeting on the campus of the University of Minnesota, Duluth. It was Valentines Day and she was there with another boy, but when she turned around and looked at me, I saw those beautiful Irish eyes, and it was all over. We sang songs and had a nice devotional but when it was time to go home, I felt depressed. After all, she had a boy friend. At least a week passed and I saw her again, and when I did, we hugged each other, and the relationship was born that would last a life time. What a different relationship Hosea had with his wife. She was a prostitute and Hosea was told that she was to be his wife. Hosea must have felt very foolish, rejected, and angry. Why did God command and allow this relationship?

Focus Scripture: Hosea 1:2

> When the Lord first spoke through Hosea, the Lord said to Hosea, "Go, take to yourself a wife of harlotry, and have children of harlotry, for the land commits flagrant harlotry, forsaking the Lord."

Focus Scripture: Hosea 1:10

> Yet the number of the sons of Israel will be like the sand of the sea which cannot be measured or numbered; and it will come about that,

in the place where it is said to them, "You are not My people," it will be said to them, "You are the sons of the living God."

Focus Scripture: Hosea 2:19

"And I will betroth you to me forever. I will betroth you to me in righteousness and in justice, in steadfast love and in mercy. I will betroth you to me in faithfulness. And you shall know the Lord."

Focus Scripture: Hosea 2:23

And I will sow her for Myself in the land. I will also have compassion on her who had not obtained compassion. And I will say to those who were not My people, "You are my people!" And they will say, "Thou art my God!"

Hosea is prophesying through his strained (yet ordained) relationship with his wife, Gomer. Here is a parallel between the broken relationship of mankind and the bridegroom, Christ. Christ deserved a perfect people to call to salvation. Instead, He took the harlot and the children of the harlot, and He forged an iron clad mechanism where the undeserving bride was reconciled to Himself.

Hosea's wife was the outcast of society, deserving of nothing but disease and death. So it was with Israel, which fell into captivity, hundreds of years before Judah. Both the person of Gomer and Israel were cut off from God, by their own choosing. As the plan for marital restoration was stated, so was the prophesy of Christ's coming.

Sometimes I joke with Susan and say "we are not related—you are my wife." One thought that is not a joke is the miracle that we are together. Think of this: two people, unrelated, coming together in a binding relationship that surpasses blood. Every paycheck, item in our home, or any blessing belongs to us, as a couple. Susan knows that I will always love her, unconditionally, and I can embrace that same security. But, in the case of our marriage to God, we are undeserving, filthy, people of harlotry. Yet, through Christ, we are taken into a heavenly family and given the right to be called "heirs of God and fellow heirs with Christ." (Romans 8:17)

Why did God chose a sinful race to be included in the plan of salvation?

Does the scripture indicate anywhere that Gomer changed from what she was into a faithful and pure wife? What may we conclude about this present generation of Christians?

Day 55: A day of clouds and thick darkness

Scripture: Joel 1:1 to 2:2

Ten to thirty million: That is the number of plant and animal species estimated to exist on our planet. According to Dan Olson (University of Minnesota), every year 50,000 species are lost to extinction. These organisms include everything from Passenger Pigeons to microorganisms. According to the Science Daily (Jan. 10, 2002), half of all living bird and mammal species will be gone in 200 to 300 years. The very soil we trod on may change as plants, microorganisms, and animals impact how mineral and nutrient content is stored. Some species will over-perform but this could have a negative impact on us. Will the whistle blow tomorrow or will it blow 300 years from now? No one knows for sure but the prophet, Joel, knows that it will blow and it will be a horrible day for some people. Try as we will (and should) to avoid the calamity of our existence on this miraculous planet, there will come a day of reconciliation and accountability.

Focus Scripture: Joel 1:3

Tell your children of it and let your children tell their children, and their children another generation.

Focus Scripture: Joel 1: 14

> Consecrate a fast, proclaim a solemn assembly; gather the elders and all the inhabitants of the land to the house of the Lord your God, and cry out to the Lord.

Focus Scripture: Joel 2:2

> A day of darkness and gloom, a day of clouds and thick darkness, as the dawn is spread over the mountains, so there is a great and mighty people; there has never been anything like it, nor will there be again after them through the years of all generations.

The parallels of Joel's prophetic words are three fold: First, there will be a time when we literally wear out the earth. Depletion of our resources and the increase of harmful organisms is inevitable. Second, there probably will be a military power that will rise up against Israel and many nations will be pulled into a conflict. The locusts of Joel could be pointing to a smashing army. Finally, we should be wary of the things that consume us, spiritually. The "organisms" of our culture may be eating away at our spiritual awareness of God's purpose for being here. Could it be that we have seen the personal "extinction" of good habits being replaced with destructive, self-serving causes?

Is there any joy in this message? It seems that the toothpaste has already left the tube and there is no turning back as we head toward Bob Dylan's "Eve of Destruction." I would only say that I would rather be with others who are on the right side, assembling together and sounding praises to the glory of God, than to slide into a state of despair. But, we must protect our minds and tune into the good things of God, and not dwell on the degradation of society. We need to sound the horn in warning without jumping out of the vehicle.

Are there things we watch on television or language that we accept that we used to shun?

Do we "cry out to the Lord" as stated in Joel 1:14 or do we simply cry? How can assembling with other Christians enable us to stay spiritually healthy?

Why does God set a plan in motion that seems so destructive and unloving?

Why do we "dry up" spiritually?

Why do churches "dry up" spiritually?

Day 56: Help me with my load

Scripture: Amos 1:1 to 2:16

We were taking an evening ride one summer and slowed down to look at a house that was for sale. I saw a pick-up truck behind me and tried to move over to the right side of the road. One could hear the disgust in the young driver's engine as he quickly tooled his truck around me. Suddenly a small white dog appeared, perhaps in pursuit of the truck. As quickly as the dog appeared, the rear tire smashed the animal in the head. My wife stroked its body as life leaked from the small skull. The left eye remained open and bulging out as it died on the asphalt that evening. The owner of the dog came running out and was overcome with emotion. The driver of the truck was struck with sorrow and regret. We all were saddened and had trouble sleeping because of the incident.

Focus Scripture: Amos 1:11,12

'This is what the Lord says: "For the three sins (or rebellions) of Edom, even four, I will not turn back my wrath because he pursued his brother with a sword, stifling all compassion, because his anger raged continually and his fury flamed unchecked, I will send fire upon Teman that will consume the fortresses of Bozrah."'

Focus Scripture: Amos 2: 13,14

> "Now then, I will crush you as a cart crushes when loaded with grain, the swift will not escape, the strong will not muster their strength, and the warrior will not save his life."

When sin finally claims a soul, whose fault is it? Is it the family, like the owners of a dog? Is it the circumstances, like those caused by the driver of the car. Or, is it the sin of someone else, like the driver of the pick-up truck. Was I at fault for slowing down, making the driver behind me angry? Figurative as the illustration is, do we interfere with others and cause them to make a decision to sin?

Usually if we sin, repent, and make a commitment not to sin again (even though we fail), there is atonement for that kind of sin. The sins of Edom were much greater than that. These were the kind of sins that were continual as illustrated in the "three...even four" phrase. Finally, there were circumstances that caused that sin to become deadly. In our shallow minds we think that the penalty of doing wrong is much too severe. After all, it was a cute little dog that just ran out after cars once in a while. We reach an impasse: it does not matter what force caused the sin...what matters is that sin results in complete destruction and death. As I read the Old Testament I realize that the reason there are so many portions of scripture devoted to the downfall of Judah and Israel is that God wants repentance and a change in behavior. If we get tired of this message, then maybe it is time we hear it again.

One of the Focus Scriptures refers to being crushed by a cart loaded with grain as well as someone who is strong but cannot escape. The illustration seems to point towards a position of being well off and self-sufficient with plenty of grain (or money) and ample strength (intelligence and resourcefulness). Yet, we can be crushed by our own self-dependency. It happens to many people who may think that they have accomplished everything and are now on the top of the heap. Truth is, they are crushed under the heap, not really knowing what God would have for their lives.

Our message is to look for ways to help our brothers and sisters in Christ and not esteem ourselves above them. We sin and cause destruction of both ourselves and others unless we reach out and minister to those in need.

What burden do we put on ourselves?

What benefit is there in reaching out to others in need?

When our jobs seem to be boring, our efforts in school futile, our marriages dull, our friendships fading, what has to change?

Is it sin to drift away from people we love? Is it love that causes us to renew our relationships?

Day 57: Repair the Chinese Lantern

Scripture: Obadiah

Riddle time: What do (or did) Mickey Mantle and Duluth's former "Chinese Lantern" have in common?

First some background. The Chinese Lantern was literally known all over the state of Minnesota and parts of Canada as one of the finest restaurants in the upper Midwest. When it burned down, people wrote letters to the owner, sent him money, and even wept, because this restaurant was a landmark for over 35 years.

Mickey Mantle was the Yankee ball player that even the jealous anti-Yankee fans admired. People would go to the ball park to see a legend, Mickey Mantle, play ball. Some sports writers said that Mantle was even more powerful than Babe Ruth. But the "Mick" gave into the social pressures of the time and drank heavily. Years later, his liver was destroyed and a transplant was necessary. Cancer was found on his liver; the doctors thought they removed it all but the cells metastasized onto Mantle's lungs and he was dead in a few months.

I visited the burned out Chinese lantern. There was no part of the interior that looked untouched by the flame that ripped through it. But I was there to assess the asbestos problem and the removal of the charred stucco and pipe insulation from the building. As we shined a light into the empty chasms of the second floor there was something of a splinter of hope.

Focus Scripture: Obadiah 1:4

> "Though you build high like the eagle, though you set your nest among the stars, from there I will bring you down," declares the Lord.

Focus Scripture: Obadiah 1:17a

> "But on Mount Zion there will be those who escape..."

Focus Scripture: Obadiah 1:21

> The deliverers will ascend Mount Zion to judge the mountain of Esau, and the kingdom will be the Lord's.

The descendants of Esau were the Edomites. Esau was the haughty, strong brother of Jacob who could do everything well. Edom assumed the personality of Esau and ridiculed the existence of Israel and appeared to be overpowering. But the time came for Edom to be overrun, for the Chinese Lantern to be destroyed, for Mantle to destroy his liver with alcohol.

When I peered through the darkness of the Chinese Lantern I saw a firm concrete beam, several of them supporting the most rudimentary structure of the building. There was also a wooden bridge that extended over the former fish pond at the entry of the restaurant. There was, indeed, something left to build on. Before Mickey Mantle died, he accepted Christ as his personal savior. In spite of his lofty times as a baseball icon, he realized that the structure of his body was totally "burned out" with cancer. Today, he is my brother in Christ in heaven.

The Chinese Lantern re-located but was never the same. The burned out building was repaired but was never again the restaurant that so many people used to visit. But, in the case of Mickey Mantle, God decided that he could have one more chance and that was the healing of a baseball great. The healing was a spiritual one but a permanent repair of a man that was a total physical loss. God looks at our burned out lives, and sees the potential for us to start over if we commit or re-dedicate ourselves to the Carpenter who can restore us all.

Are there areas of our lives where we think that we have built a protected nest, like the eagle referred to in Obadiah 1:4?

Is a burn-out necessary or are there ways to avoid physical and spiritual destruction?

The last verse of Obadiah says "Deliverers will go up to Mount Zion in Jerusalem to rule over the Mountains of Edom. And the Lord himself will be King." What does this mean and when will it occur?

Record your thoughts about the prophetic words found in verse 17. "But Jerusalem will become a refuge for those who escape; it will be a holy place. And the people of Israel will come back to reclaim their inheritance."

Day 58: Could you please tell me where I am?

Scripture: Jonah 1:1 to 2:10

Most have heard the familiar story of Jonah and think of it as a mythical recording of a great whale swallowing a man and then regurgitating him on the shoreline. Actually, the story has much deeper meaning and extended lessons about repentance and obeying God in all circumstances.

I was in Lagos, Nigeria, working as a geologist and one weekend I got a little bored and decided to take the car out. It was not recommended that I drive the car and only a hired national was supposed to drive the vehicle. This company policy was designed to protect the company employees from dangerous situations. But, I decided to go my own way and when I was routed onto a road, I realized that I was going the wrong direction and I needed to turn around as soon as possible or I would end up on a dangerous street in downtown Lagos.

Focus Scripture: Jonah 1:8-9

> "What have you done to bring this awful storm down on us?" they demanded. "Who are you? What is your line of work? What country are you from? What is your nationality?" And Jonah answered, "I am a Hebrew, and I worship the Lord, the God of heaven, who made the sea and the land."

Focus Scripture: Jonah 2:5

> Water encompassed me to the point of death. The great deep engulfed me, weeds were wrapped around my head.

Focus Scripture: Jonah 2:7-9

> When I had lost all hope, I turned my thoughts once more to the Lord. And my earnest prayer went out to you in your holy Temple. Those who worship false gods turn their backs on all God's mercies. But I will sacrifice to You with songs of praise, and I will fulfill my vows. For my salvation comes from the Lord alone.

It is unfortunate that we tend to wait until there is a raging storm in our lives before we "turn our thoughts once more to the Lord." But, we all tend to do that to a greater or lesser extent. It is not just about us messing up ourselves, it is about messing up others who may be examining our blueprint to living.

The day I was in downtown Lagos and lost, I asked a commercial motorcycle driver to guide me out of the crowded streets and back home. He took a friend on the back of his motorcycle and started to lead me out of the congested area. I was a little frightened because I did not think that he needed that "helper" to guide me. Perhaps they would work together to find a quiet area and take my car and everything else. It turned out that they were leading me back the right way and my prayers were apparently being answered. However, when we came to an armed check-point, the police pulled the young men off the motorcycle and started beating them. The police then questioned why I was associating myself with these drug dealers. I was implicated by association and had to do some explaining. I had to confess like Jonah that I was not where I was supposed to be, state that I was sorry, and plead that the police would help me get back to home. Of course, in Lagos, that means a little gift to the police was in order but they escorted me back safely.

Sometimes we face embarrassment and humility that is unbearable. The irony of this is that we can repent and get back on track, becoming even stronger than before. I changed my prayer about my safety to a prayer about the motorcycle driver and his friend. I will never know if the police were truthful about these young men but I knew that they were the ones who were in trouble and needed God's help. When Jonah finally delivered his message at Nineveh, he had doubts about the results and we can identify with that, not knowing how our missions will impact others. But, we can be assured that our words and actions will be directed to the right people if we are obedient.

Does God know when we will be disobedient?

Does forgiveness give us license to run our lives the way we want, knowing that God will come to the rescue if we cry out to Him?

Why was Job disobedient in the first place? Can we recognize these reasons and learn from them without ending up in bad circumstances?

Day 59: Is there peace in the valley?

Scripture: Micah 4:1-13; 5:1-5

"Peace" is a word that means different things to different people. Some would declare that we enjoyed a period of peace between the Korean War and the Viet Nam war but the cold war was hardly peaceful. Peace can come in inexpensive packages or in very expensive vacations. My father-in-law used to talk about the wonderful peace he enjoyed by the Lester River (Duluth, MN). He often talked about the canopy of White Pines hovering over the continuous music of the stream. As a young man I recall similar experiences in the evening next to Lake Adelaide in Northeastern Wisconsin, listening to the cackle of the loons as the silver water glistened beneath the moon. That was real peace, at least until the mosquitoes decided to dine. Years later, I would gaze at my son sleeping in the arms of my smiling wife, enjoying the peaceful look of our baby and the sparkling eyes of his mother. All these moments of peace are temporary, and as beautiful as they are, they are fleeing moments. For lasting peace, we look to Bethlehem.

Focus Scripture: Micah 4:3

> He will judge between many peoples and will settle disputes for strong nations far and wide. They will beat their swords into plowshares and their spears into pruning hooks. Nation will not take up sword against nation, nor will they train for war anymore.

Earl Fashbaugh

Focus Scripture: Micah : 4, 5

> ...And He shall stand and feed His flock in the strength of the Lord, in the Majesty of the name of the Lord His God, and His people will remain there undisturbed, for He will be greatly honored in all the world. He will be our peace. And when the Assyrian invades our land, and marches across our hills, he will appoint seven shepherds to watch over us, eight princes to lead us.

My father-in-law lost his wife to Alzheimer's Disease. My son grew up and is faced with financial struggles as he raises three beautiful sons of his own. The lake I once gazed at is still there but I had to move on to other responsibilities. We can enjoy peace of the moment but we can be enthralled in the peace of knowing that God will protect us and love us, unconditionally. When we know the peace of a moment along with the peace of God, we can lock something into our hearts that no one can take away. We will be invaded by the "Assyrians" of this life. They may come with financial disaster, failing health, overwhelming disappointments, and even death. But the real peace is still vivid and encompassing, granting us security in knowing that our Comforter is ultimately the one who created the stream, the sleeping baby, and the canopy of stars. When we come to a point of knowing this, our strength is renewed, daily, and we feel the presence of the Great Shepherd.

Recall the most wonderful moment in your life and think of what it was like without God and now think of it with God. What is the difference?

Micah witnessed the fall of a large portion of the Nation Israel and yet he prophesied peace. How could peace and destruction possibly coexist?

Day 60: Yes, there is peace in the valley

Scripture: Nahum 1:1 to 1:15

It was a joyous day. The wind was brisk, out of the north, and occasional gusts were laden with sleet. It was June 15, 1974, the day that Susan Monroe gave her hand in marriage to Earl Fashbaugh. For me, it was the most beautiful day of my life, because, on that day, my childhood dream came true. The vows we made stand today and I renew them daily with a prayer. The day we were married, it was a day of liberation from loneliness and a life commitment to the great sacrament of marriage. This same experience is offered to us by God. On the one hand we become bound to Him, but on the other hand we become free from fear. We no longer doubt our purpose. We grab onto His hand which will lead us onto our rightful home.

But wait. Are we really free from fear? Do we not have to look up in the heavens and think about the Universe winding down. Our earth is precarious, perfectly positioned and mass-balanced to support all the life and water on this planet. Change anything, even a little, and the water could be turned to steam or the ice caps could grow and reach the equator. Depending on the reader of these prophesies, we will either be "scared to hell" or driven to Love.

Focus Scripture: Nahum 1: 3-4

> The lord is slow to anger and great in power; the Lord will not leave the guilty unpunished. His way is in the whirlwind and the storm, and clouds are the dust of his feet. He rebukes the sea and dries it up; he makes all the rivers run dry.

Focus Scripture: Nahum 1:15

> See the messengers running down the mountains with glad (good) news: "The invaders have been wiped out and we are safe." O Judah, Proclaim the day of Thanksgiving, and worship only the Lord, as you have vowed. For this enemy from Nineveh will never come again. He is cut off forever; he will never be seen again.

Nahum's message to Nineveh eventually came true. Jonah warned this ungodly people and they turned to God for about 100 years but they eventually succumbed to sinful ways. There are no safe places to hide outside of God even though our society may plead that we are in control and worth all the niceties of the 21st century.

When I go to sleep at night and kiss my wife, I know that she will be there for me the next day and she has the same assurance. One day, she or I will be gone and we will have to face the grim reality of growing old apart. But, we have the creator of the stream that carries living water up and down our souls to give us the kind of peace that surpasses all understanding (Philippians 4:7).

The parallels of marriage to our relationship with Christ are striking. The parallel breaks down when it comes to physical death. We therefore must cling to our vows with the Lord because that relationship cannot be terminated. The "invaders" of this life may try to take our peace and security away, but they will never succeed. Every day should be a day of Thanksgiving and worship. The messengers still run down the mountain and proclaim the good news that we are free; that any dark thoughts will not dictate our well being.

Why did God send Jonah to Nineveh if He was going to destroy the entire city anyway?

How do we fear and love God simultaneously?

Are there any other verses in Nahum that strike you personally? Take a snapshot and record your thoughts.

Day 61: God, what are you doing?

Scripture: Habakkuk 1:1 to 2:3

In North America, we have several options that allow us to live a variety of lifestyles. We can change jobs, return to college, or become active in any number of civic groups. Even in the midst of economic downturns, we enjoy a high standard of living by world standards. The nation of Judah once enjoyed this kind of security, but moral decline and corruption brought the country to a point of spiritual impoverishment. The question that Habakkuk asked is a timeless one: "Why, God, do you allow evil to happen to good people?"

Focus Scripture: Habakkuk 1:13

Your eyes are too pure to look on evil; you cannot tolerate wrong. Why then do you tolerate the treacherous? Why are you silent while the wicked swallow up those more righteous than themselves?

Focus Scripture: Habakkuk 2:1

I will stand at my watch and station myself on the ramparts. I will look to see what he will say to me, and what answer I am to give to this complaint.

Focus Scripture: Habakkuk 2:2-3

> Then the Lord replied: "Write down the revelation and make it plain on tablets so that a herald may run with it. For revelation awaits an appointed time; it speaks of the end and will not prove false. Though it linger, wait for it; it will certainly come and will not delay."

It seems odd that anyone would have a disagreement with God. But, we all have this conversation with God at some time or another. A modern conversation may go like this:

Habakkuk: God, what is going on here? Weren't we the chosen and blessed nation of America? Why have you allowed such corrupt organizations to run our institutions? Pornography and disease are running rampant and yet the perpetrators of corruption are free to do as they wish.

God: Huck, let me ask you the same question, why? If you would just quit whining and look at what you did instead of what I allowed...

Habakkuk: That's not a fair response. Look at what has happened to us. Please, God, rescue us and put an end to this captivity by evil perpetrators.

God: You will see destruction of the ungodly like you have never seen before. They reign a short while but the spiritualists, child exploiters, and the terrorists will face a horrible demise that you cannot imagine.

Habakkuk: I am going to sit here until you answer me straight.

God: That's good that you are standing guard and listening but you may have missed something that I said...

The dialogue continues in Chapter 3 when Habakkuk realizes the provisions for those who love Him are just as genuine as they were from the beginning. The great deliverance of His people is matched by the horrible destruction of evil. Still, the warning is perched like a vulture, salivating at the feast that comes from consuming a nation that succumbs to moral degradation.

The question we tend to ask is, "why is my glass half empty" or "why is my glass only half full." The real question we need to ask is, "why has God allowed there to be anything in the glass at all?" We see a world where people are killing each other and mocking God, taking Him out of our government and schools, and completely denying His existence. We forget that He has allowed us to choose in the context of His ultimate blueprint of the Universe. He hears us but we often do not hear Him.

A friend of mine came up to me after church and said, "God has really been speaking to me, lately." He had been going through a struggle with teen-age boys and was subject to the stress of living in a new community and working at a different job. He was experiencing peace about his circumstances. All I could say was, "you mean God was not speaking to you before?" Perhaps we are like people who storm into God's office when we pray and tell Him what is wrong, instead of humbly knocking at His door and praising Him for what is right.

How is Obadiah's (Day 58) or Jonah's (Day 59) message similar or different from Habakkuk's?

How does God react to us grumbling to Him? Should we complain to Him?

Day 62: Mind the signs

Scripture: Zephaniah 1:1 to 2:7

When I was a boy, we learned about the evils of air pollution in science class but the impact was not taught as it were a global concern. Still, everyone suspected that the fruits of the industrial revolution were not all good. But, we were hooked on comfort, whether in an air conditioned car or in a heated garage. Our first indication that we were having a global impact on the environment came from reports that the ozone layer was breaking down. We were to learn that refrigerants leaked out of cooling units and caused a decline in upper atmospheric ozone. We further learned that carbon dioxide and methane were causing heat to be trapped beneath the frail atmosphere. The feed-back loop would suggest that other environmental problems could threaten us more than the extinction of polar bears. But, before our human race is threatened, there will be changes in the economy and how international business systems function. How do or will we respond to these warnings? How did the people of Zephaniah's day respond to his prophetic warnings?

Focus Scripture: Zephaniah 1:11-14

> Wail, you who live in the market district; all you merchants will be wiped out, all who trade with silver will be ruined...Their wealth will be plundered, their houses demolished. They will build houses but not live in them; they will plant vineyards but not drink the wine.

That terrible day is near. Swiftly it comes – a day when strong men will weep bitterly.

Focus Scripture: Zephaniah 1:18

Neither their silver nor their gold will be able to save them on the day of the Lord's wrath. In the fire of jealousy the whole world will be consumed, for he will make a sudden end of all who live in the earth.

Focus Scripture: Zephaniah 2:1

Gather together and pray, you shameless nation, while there still is time – before judgment begins, and your opportunity is blown away like chaff; before the fierce anger of the Lord falls and the terrible day of his wrath begins.

Focus Scripture: Zephaniah 2:3

Seek the Lord, all you humble of the land, you who do what He commands. Seek righteousness, seek humility; perhaps you will be sheltered on the day of the Lord's anger.

Focus Scripture: Zephaniah 2:7

There the little remnant of the tribe of Judah will be pastured. They will lie down to rest in the abandoned houses in Ashkelon. For the Lord God will visit his people in kindness and restore their prosperity again.

These verses were written between 520 and 518 BC. Yet, the warnings could well be phrased in a manner consistent with a Wall Street Journal editorial. For example, Zephaniah 1:13 could read "foreclosures are rampant and creditors are pulling out of commitments for large construction projects, often leaving shopping Malls with nothing more than cinder blocks and concrete slabs."

In the midst of today's drama we see signs: "The end is near," "get ready to meet thy God," "the world is ending." And, if the world does not end today, the signs will be good tomorrow, or the next day. So, when Zephaniah wrote in verse 14, "the great day of the Lord is near" people may have looked around and saw prosperity and they had their doubts about this prophesy. After 2500 years, the world has not ended. In fact, we have found cures for diseases, the information age is at our finger tips, and we enjoy a standard of living that few people could ever aspire to. But, in God's eyes, Zephaniah's prophesy could be yesterday and the stability of our planet is only temporary.

But, there is hope found in verse 2:3. The scripture instructs us to seek the Lord and do what He commands and "perhaps you will be sheltered on the day of the Lord's anger." The implications here are that we can really screw up but can avoid severe punishment if we return to living within the confines of God's Law.

In Minnesota we are proud of our bad winter driving conditions. At times the entire state is covered with slippery roads. There have been times when our family would stop and eat lunch at a restaurant and wait for reports from truck drivers. If we heard one driver say that the roads were bad, that would cause us to take head. If another driver reports the same thing, we start to re-think our plans. If still another driver reports cars in the ditch and very tough conditions ahead, we re-route our course. Our "snapshot" of the Bible suggests that there are an incredible number of truck drivers, called "minor prophets" that come into our restaurant with the same message: IF YOU CONTINUE TO GO IN THE SAME DIRECTION, YOU WILL GO IN THE DITCH OR MUCH WORSE!

Zephaniah 2:1 says, "Gather together and pray" as a solution to our individual and national problems. This togetherness is an instruction that must not be denied. Collective prayer strengthens our resolve and affirms our positive feelings while diminishing our negative feelings. A well trained soldier standing in the middle of a battle field by himself is very vulnerable but a regiment of soldiers becomes a formidable force. So it is with the power of prayer.

If the world ends, how can we possibly be sheltered on the "day of the Lord?"

As a result of Zephaniah's prophesy, King Josiah became a leader that followed the commandments of God and Judah was protected from her adversaries. Could the same happen today if leaders sought righteousness?

What does Zephaniah mean when he writes "neither silver or gold will be able to save them?"

The alternative to taking a bad road is sometimes to wait. If we wait, what should we be doing in the meantime?

Day 63: Help wanted; no experience

Scripture Haggai 1:1 to 2:23 (Living Bible)

When I first recorded my personal snapshots of the book of Haggai, there was little money in our checkbook and we struggled to pay our mortgage. Our family went from a great paycheck to a little one and our savings were depleted. The kids were entering high school with several demands on the budget and I stopped and contemplated where I went wrong. I wondered if I had violated the will of God and because of it I was being punished with poverty.

First, there is need to understand the historical context of Haggai. The Jewish nation was rebuilding after being held in captivity so there was a certain amount of splurging and celebration with what resources were at hand. Second, there was procrastination to re-build the temple. This meant that the people were hard-wiring themselves to selfish living without worship in a common place of fellowship and devotion. We must all understand that the blessings of God are free but we must get our spiritual house in order and attend to building our relationship with God and others.

Focus Scripture: Haggai 1:6

> Your income disappears as though you were putting it into pockets filled with holes.

Focus Scripture: Haggai 1: 14, 15

> And the Lord gave them a desire to rebuild His temple, so they all gathered in early September of the second year of King Darius' reign, and volunteered their help.

Focus Scripture: Haggai 2:14

> Haggai then made his meaning clear. "You people," he said (speaking for the Lord) "were contaminating your sacrifices by living with selfish attitudes and evil hearts – and not only your sacrifices, but everything else that you did as a service to me."

We need to make a spiritual reality check every once in a while. When we do this, we re-direct our resources to more worthwhile causes. These resources could be financial but could also be in the form of serving. We serve by swerving, steering clear of the things that divert constructive relationships with people we love. An email of encouragement or a Thank You card of love can make a big difference in other people's lives and those acts of love bounce right back at us. Look at this list of contrasting decisions:

I could watch a questionable show	OR	I will help clean up the kitchen
I could read my novel.	OR	I will restructure my spending plan
I could get ready for fantasy football	OR	I will study for a Sunday School Lesson
I could go out for coffee and pie	OR	I will visit the nursing home
I could take a pleasure drive	OR	I will help organize the garage

Can we climb out of literal and spiritual poverty by re-directing our efforts? Certainly on a spiritual level, we can. And, I would contend, that if we position our priorities to serve others, especially in our families, we will better utilize our material resources, making the paycheck stretch a little further. We may even find physical and spiritual resources that we did not know we had.

How often and to what extent should we make a spiritual reality check?

Take a snapshot of your financial situation and try to understand where your efforts are directed. What areas could you improve in?

Make your own columns up of negative and re-directed efforts to better serve God and family

<u>I could</u>   OR   <u>I will</u>

Day 64: So, we're in a recession

Scripture: Zechariah (1:1-21)

When I started writing "Snapshots" in 1991, the first Gulf war was over and the U.S. appeared to be the Super Power of the World. It was clear that America ruled militarily, financially, and productively. Desert Storm was an invasion that demonstrated resolve and commitment to democracy, liberating Kuwait from the stronghold of the Iraq Army. Trust in America soared and other countries yielded with respect to declarations of the United States. Patriotism was everywhere and it appeared that America could do no wrong.

Times have changed since then. At this writing, the economy is in shambles and homes are being foreclosed at an alarming rate. The U.S. is trying to leave Iraq after a second invasion but it is difficult to leave with confidence that Iraq will be able to stand as a unified country. An entire generation removed from the first Gulf War is looking at an economic crisis in America, not witnessed since the Great Depression. The once confident image of America has been displaced with doubt and skepticism, at least among the other nations.

Recessions (and even Depressions) will come and go but through each of them we can learn and return to a way of life that depends on prayer and God's mercy. When an entire nation does this, confidence is restored and economic growth is renewed. But, do we really learn from those hard times or do we forget the storm that we have endured? The message of Zechariah is one of returning to a God who is jealous for our devotion and if it takes a rough cycle to get us back to Him, then it is reassuring that we are loved Children, wayward as we may be.

Focus Scripture: Zechariah 1:2-4

The Lord who rules over all was very angry with our people years ago. And now he says to us, "Return to me. Then I will return to you," announces the Lord. "Do not be like your people years ago. The earlier prophets gave them my message. I said, 'Stop doing what is evil. Turn away from your sinful practices.' But they would not listen to me. They would not pay any attention," announces the Lord.

Focus Scripture: Zechariah 1:5-6

"Where are those people now? And what about my prophets? Do they live forever? I commanded my servants the prophets what to say. I told them what I planned to do. But your people refused to obey me. So I had to punish them." Then they had a change of heart. They said, 'The Lord who rules over all has punished us because of how we have lived. He was fair and right to do that. He has done to us just what he decided to do.'

Focus Scripture: Zechariah 1:16

So the Lord says, "I will return to Jerusalem. I will show its people my tender love. My temple will be rebuilt there. Workers will use a measuring line when they rebuild Jerusalem," announces the Lord. He says, "My towns will be filled with good things once more. I will comfort Zion. And I will choose Jerusalem again."

God has not forgotten the Jewish people anymore than He has forgotten the United States. But, there is a personal message here; one that is reduced to our individual relationship to God. Unless we move towards Him in our everyday activities, we will lose confidence in the creation He made in us. We will grow weak and spiritually famished and seem to lack purpose unless our whole lives focus on the One who loves us more than anyone else.

The focus scripture suggests that God administers punishment. This is amazing when we think about it. The God of the entire Universe could just let our actions go without admonishing us. We would, after all, punish ourselves and justice would prevail. But, because He loves us so much, he actually inflicts punishment. We must conclude that God would not admonish us if there was not some kind of plan or purpose that God wants us to realize. Secondly, God wants us to be happy in Him. The blessing of a Holy Father are waiting for us but we must move to the place where the blessings are waiting. Punishment can lead to blessings.

Far be it from us to understand the scope of God's Universal Plan. We can only try to understand and use illustrations of a parent acting quickly to divert undesirable behavior. My four year old son ran ahead of me one time after I told him to wait. He pulled away from my hand and started to run across the street. I ran quickly to keep him from darting out into the busy street. It was one of those few times that I swatted him on the butt and gave him a lecture on safety. Then, I hugged my only son and kissed his little blonde head as we both had tears. God is like that. He loves us enough to grab us and take a paddle to our behavior in order to protect us spiritually and (sometimes) physically.

Then there is Jesus who ran ahead of us all and knowingly let himself get run over by the punishing traffic of humankind. He took our punishment so that we could be safe (and saved).

In what ways have we made God jealous?

As you read the first 18 verses of Zechariah, what personal message does God reveal to you?

If you had one day left to live, what would you do?

Earl Fashbaugh

Does God punish us? Why should He when He created us the way we are?

The Bible has examples of free well and predestination. What does this snapshot suggest?

Day 65: Your best used tennis shoes

Scripture: Malachi 1: 1-13

We refer to the day as simply, "911." Everyone recalls September 11th, the day that terrorists hijacked four planes and flew two of them into the World Trade Center in New York. My wife and I were in Nigeria when someone came into my office and told me that "America was going up in smoke." I went home and turned on CNN and was shocked with the rest of the world to see buildings collapse before my eyes. History was recorded vividly as we watched in slow motion, the jet entering one of the buildings and a fireball coming out the other side. I wanted to be home in America on that day to join hands in prayer with other Americans in the face of the worst terrorist activity that my country has ever experienced. Church attendance in the U.S. jumped up from 41% to 47% and the resolve of American strength, spiritually and otherwise, was evident. But, by November, not even three months later, attendance was back down to 42%.

Malachi was written around 460 to 430 BC. Malachi was the last prophet before John the Baptist heralded the coming of Jesus. It was a time of despair and spiritual carelessness where some people would go through the motions of religious sacrifice but would bring animals to the altar that were sick, diseased, or even stolen livestock. They would then walk away thinking that they had blessed God and were off the hook from any spiritual responsibility. They gave superstitiously and not supernaturally and the Jewish faith appeared to be tumbling into the ruins of time. People were worshiping themselves and had compromised every sacred oath of their faith.

Focus Scripture Malachi 1:1

> Israel, I, the LORD, have loved you. And yet you ask, "in what way have I loved you?"

Focus Scripture: Malachi 1:7

> You embarrass me by offering worthless food on my altar. Then you ask, "How have we embarrassed you?" You have done it by saying, "What's so great about the LORD's altar?"

Focus Scripture: Malachi 1:8

> But isn't it wrong to offer animals that are blind, crippled, or sick? Just try giving those animals to your governor.

Focus Scripture: Malachi 1:13-14

> You get so disgusted that you even make vulgar signs at me. And for an offering, you bring stolen animals or those that are crippled or sick. Should I accept these? Instead of offering the acceptable animals you have promised, you bring me those that are unhealthy.

I have three pairs of tennis shoes. My newest and best shoes are used primarily to play racquetball. Another pair is used for casual wear when out and about and sometimes for running or walking. My third pair is for working around the yard. The last pair is just one day away from the garbage but I keep them in order to preserve my best shoes. All of these shoes start out as racquetball shoes and "work" their way down to smelly yard shoes. If God asked me to run a marathon and wear a good pair of shoes that would endure, I would certainly wear my best, racquetball shoes and not the torn, dirty, smelly sneakers. We are all asked today to put on the best shoes we have and run the marathon. We have to decide how we will show up in front of our coach. Will we be rested, clean, and with our best foot wear on? Will we give all we can? Or, will we shortchange ourselves and our Creator?

How are we similar today to the Jewish people during Malachi's time?

Are there areas where we have compromised the commandments of God?

Are there signs in our society that imply that God is no longer welcome in our public institutions?

What does God expect from us? What areas of our lives should we examine in terms of giving to God?

The terrorist attack of 911 was a tragic reminder that forces of evil are allowed to roam the earth. These unleashed forces cause us to ask questions about how much God is involved in preventing such atrocities. For what ever reason, we are asked to respond to the tragedies of our nation or of our lives. We can shake our fists at God or we can sit down with Him through the person of Jesus Christ. The United States stood unified behind the truths of an American heritage for three months and then returned to a more secular existence. Lip service does not go very far in changing a nation or changing the people who live in it. Prosperity does not cause us to want to be a blessing to God. In fact, some of the poorest countries in the world have greater church attendance than America. Point in case, Nigeria has an 89% weekly, church attendance rate. You will often find Nigerians reading their Bible, taking notes, and preparing for Sunday School. Nigerian Christians will sometimes make church an all-day event because it is the highlight and delight of their lives. God would like us to approach His altar with an attitude of giving the best of ourselves out of deep and abiding love. This love far exceeds percentages of income and causes total commitment from a pure heart.

Day 66: Late but not too late

Scripture: Revelations 1:1-20

One of my favorite pictures is that of my daughter in her wedding dress, smiling radiantly as the morning sunshine. The sparkle in her eyes testifies to the happiness of a bride with her wonderful husband. As a father, I feel the same joy, knowing that my precious little girl is off on a voyage with the man God chose for her. I see a story in her that stretches from the first day I held her in my arms to the time when she will one day be a delightful mother. Revelation is that kind of book that pulls the ancient prophecies to the present and lets us gaze into the future and see the Lord of Lords come to take his bride (the church) to stand by His side. The difference here is that there will be times that are not so wonderful in the future when the very words on this page will be consumed by fire.

John was a tired old man with a leathery face and scarred hands, testifying to his early life as a professional fisherman. The prison was damp and sometimes hot but always miserable. It had been well over 60 years since he last saw Jesus. Churches had been planted, souls were saved, a revolution was underway, people were liberated, but he was in prison because Rome did not want this new religion to cause upheaval. John was near the end of his life, but he was writing about the beginning and the end at the same time; the first and the last, the alpha and the omega, the God who was there at creation and will always be there after all hell breaks loose (literally) on our frail planet.

Focus Scripture: Revelation 1: 10, 11

> "On the Lord's Day I was in the Spirit, and I heard behind me a loud voice like a trumpet, which said: 'Write on a scroll what you see and send it to the seven churches: to Ephesus, Smyrna, Pergamum, Thyatira Sardis, Philadelphia and Laodicea.'"

Focus Scripture: Revelation 1:17b-18

> "Do not be afraid, I am the first and the last, and the living One and I was dead, and behold, am alive forevermore, and I have the keys to death and of Hades."

My wife locked the keys in the car several years ago. After several phone calls she connected with a locksmith who finally got her into the car. He was quite a welcome site to my desperate wife who was 200 miles from home.

Revelation is a Book about keys and getting a locksmith in order to get into a vehicle that has been parked in the garden of Eden. The car had set there since mankind locked themselves out. It is a story of how mankind tried to somehow get into the vehicle. They tried a coat hanger called religion, a magnet called intellect. We even tried to squeeze a hand of goodwill into a small crack but mankind could not get back into the car. It was only when the forgiving locksmith came that there appeared an avenue back into the vehicle.

Throughout the Mediterranean, the Christian church was flourishing but not without problems. Some were forgetting their first love, Jesus. Some were socializing but not really committed to Christ, others were trying to hold onto the old religion and philosophies and add Jesus as they pleased. None of these things work. God is telling us in this book that He wants our all, our witness as well as our work; our commitment to Him.

If we act confident in our own abilities and our own self-edifying theology, we are fooling ourselves. We still remain locked out of the God-sanctioned vehicle that was manufactured for us. In Genesis, God says "Let us create man in our image, according to our likeness." When we locked ourselves out of the car, we started a search, a search that ends in Revelations. The search has taken humankind through cults, wars, famine, hurt upon hurt, and death. Our reliance on self makes us a very vulnerable target for Satan because we claim credit for our God-given abilities and lose site of the creator of the universe. Finally, Jesus makes an entry into this world and offers the plan that was initiated before the foundation of the earth. Now is the time for us to make a call to the only locksmith that can open the vehicle to everlasting life.

As we read about the seven churches in Revelation, which ones would we like to identify with and how may we be like all the seven churches?

Why did John write Revelation?

We know very little about John from the gospels. Can we conjure up how John changed as he grew older and saw the church flourish. Were the speed bumps along the way similar to those in our church today?

Concluding Remarks

Summarizing, the collection of writings that we call the Bible were assembled by people with a passion for God. These people were inspired to record actual history or to express what has been laid upon their hearts. Finally, the word of God became printed so that we all could read and understand it. There is nothing sacred about my observations. What is sacred is what God does to the heart of a person who earnestly tries to draw near to Him. The scriptures cause a person to take a snapshot of themselves and see if there is some area of their life that could be improved or to understand that Jesus provided ample Grace to overcome any and all deficiencies in our lives.

The intent of this devotional was never to scan the entire Bible but to reflect on the significance of the initial observations of the individual books. Sometimes these books are very short letters (example III John) and it is prudent to read the entire book before taking any "snapshots." In many other instances the scripture has a mammoth message at the interior or end of the Book (examples: Job, Revelation). This would necessitate going back and collecting additional "snapshots." Of course, our ultimate goal should be to study each book in its entirety and reflect on applications to society, church, family, and our lives.

The scriptures used in this book were taken from several different translations in order to serve the purpose of what was discussed in the text. Some scholars would argue against this approach but I contend that it is the dialogue between a reader and God that is important and not the precision of the translation that counts. If we record our experiences with

His Word, we will grow to understand why we are on this planet and get a glimpse of the glory that is to come. We are forever grateful for those who have given their entire existence to writing about God's Word and translating the Bible into many different languages. Ultimately, however, we have to look to what the Holy Spirit says to us as we read His Word and deal with each situation in this short life.

But, there is one portion of Revelation that cannot be skipped:

Revelation 23:7

> "Behold, I am coming soon! Blessed is he who keeps the words of the prophecy in this book."

These are the words of Jesus. He is making two very important declarations. First, He is coming, soon. And, second, we are to keep and abide by the words prophesied by Him and others who have been plugged into the will of God. Some of the prophecies are horrible and many of the Jewish prophecies seem repetitious. But, here we see Jesus stating that He is coming soon. Time can be compressed or expanded according to His definition. The repetition throughout the Bible can only emphasis His desire that we take note of our sinful nature and draw as close to God as possible in order to have complete, purposeful, meaningful, and godly lives. He is not trying to threaten us. Rather, He wants to love us.